Compliments of

BERNHARDT
WEALTH MANAGEMENT

7601 Lewinsville Road, Suite 210
McLean, VA 22102
(703) 356-4380
www.BernhardtWealth.com

Advance Praise for *Buen Camino*

"This book, like its author, is authentic, clear, and able to guide you along a pathway toward achieving goals in your portfolio and in life."

—Kristina Bouweiri, President and CEO,
Reston Limousine Service, Inc.

"Gordon Bernhardt believes in the value of wise counsel and empirical research when working with investors. He wholeheartedly sees the role of the advisor as being an enjoyable traveling companion whose only interest is to help clients arrive at their intended destination. How to get there? Buen Camino offers a useful map filled with personal insights and investment wisdom."

—David Butler, Co-CEO, Dimensional Fund Advisors

"Buen Camino is more than pages in a book or a story shared. Gordon's book is a journey in which you join and which will touch your soul. As you walk with Gordon through the pages, you find yourself asking deep and probing questions of your own life journey, how you are experiencing today, preparing for tomorrow, and yes, stopping to be aware, to be present. Rich with colorful encounters, unforeseen challenges, one senses strength in the air, accomplishment with each step, and gratitude for lessons learned. Rarely are you gifted with someone's journey so impactful to your own."

—Lynda Ellis, CEO and Owner of Capitol Concierge, Inc.

"*Reading Gordon Bernhardt's book about his walk on the Camino de Santiago is like having an interesting conversation with someone you like and trust. I know Gordon as both a respected colleague and a valued friend, and I can assure you that reading* Buen Camino *will not only make you a wiser investor— it will make you a better person.*"

—KIMBERLY FOSS, Founder and President, Empyrion Wealth Management, and *New York Times* bestselling author of *Wealthy By Design: A 5-Step Plan for Financial Security*

"Buen Camino *is a testament of Gordon's desire to experience life, gratitude for the opportunity to share his journey with others, and a faith so strong that even when faced with the challenge of the Meseta he was not deterred. Gordon is too cool to worry, and every adventure he takes contributes to his 'dash.'*"

—KATHRYN B. FREELAND, MBA, President and CEO, A-TEK, Inc.

"*From Gordon's journey, we learn walking can be good, not just for body and mind—but also for the soul. A heartfelt expression that transcends barriers between financial and spiritual wellbeing. A must-read, written from the heart. Thank you for this book!*"

—STEVE FREISHTAT, Founder and CEO, Next Day Blinds Corporation

"*It takes a writer of Gordon Bernhardt's caliber to make a story essentially based on a walk across Spain sensational. This book is truly a thrilling story of an individual's journey in the world of commerce and challenges of life. Many of us have said, 'I need to get away to think.' Gordon's pilgrimage amid the Way of St. James gave him time to grasp the responsibilities to his customers and retreat from the everyday rigors of life for spiritual growth. This book should be required reading for C-suite leadership.*"
—RADM TERRY McKNIGHT, USN (Ret), author of *Pirate Alley: Commanding Task Force 151 off the Coast of Somalia*

"*As Gordon points out in this joyous book of journey, we are all fellow travelers working in tandem toward a common goal. By staying present and open to possibilities, you'll discover within these pages the keys to legacy and purpose.*"
—SARAH E. NUTTER, PhD, University of Oregon

"*This work is from the heart! It is an uncompromisingly honest depiction of a true professional dedicated to helping others along life's journey. In his book, Gordon utilizes his adventure on the Camino de Santiago to depict and fine-tune the essence of his life's work. It reveals his focus on his clients and their needs as they transcend the many challenges of life. Most of all, this work provides a clear depiction of how he chooses to live his life in service to others. What an extremely delightful and enjoyable read with lessons to be learned by all!*"
—PHIL PANZARELLA, Serial Entrepreneur, Executive Coach, Veteran and West Point Graduate.

"*Gordon has done a masterful job using his trek as a metaphor for his philosophy about life and approach to wealth management. He reveals a rare combination of professional proficiency and personal transparency with a genuine commitment to the success of others. No matter where you are on your trajectory of life, this is good reading. I'm looking forward to sharing his insights with my CEO clients.*"

—PETER SCHWARTZ, Master Chair,
Vistage Worldwide and Fellow Peregrino

BUEN CAMINO

BUEN CAMINO

What a Hike through Spain

Taught Me about Investing and Life

Stephanie,

Buen Camino!

Gordon J Bernhardt

GORDON J.
BERNHARDT

LIONCREST
PUBLISHING

Hardcover ISBN: 978-1-5445-3222-6
Paperback ISBN: 978-1-5445-3221-9
Ebook ISBN: 978-1-5445-3220-2

To my parents, Bobby and Irene Bernhardt,
who taught me almost everything I learned on the Camino;
I just didn't know it yet.

CONTENTS

Many Roads, One Journey

July 20, 2018: Saint-Jean-Pied-de-Port, France, 7:20 a.m.

Today is the first day of the most important and meaningful undertaking I have ever attempted, and I am crouched over a toilet wishing I could throw up, but unable to manage even that. My guts feel like they've been invaded by snakes. This is not a promising start for what I'd hoped would be a transformative experience. I have journeyed here from my home in the Washington, DC area, to walk more than six hundred miles across Spain—roughly five hundred miles on the Camino de Santiago (the Way of St. James) and another hundred miles to Muxía and Finisterre on the western coast—but at this moment I can't even walk out of the bathroom.

It didn't help that I hadn't slept the night before. The heightened anticipation of beginning this journey—combined with the snoring of the other *peregrinos* (pilgrims) in the stuffy *albergue* (hostel)—kept me awake much of the night. Still, I had woken up early, dressed, put my backpack in order, and had a light breakfast, determined to begin my pilgrimage. But before I started walking, I felt sick to my stomach, and there I was in the hostel bathroom.

A part of me knew that I wasn't really sick; I was afraid. What if I couldn't make the journey? What if I had been kidding myself all this time, and this was a huge mistake? A few years ago, I had tried to make a much shorter trek, and that attempt ended in excruciating pain and failure. Why did I think I could walk six hundred miles across northern Spain?

I'll always be thankful that instead of continuing to hug that toilet in Saint-Jean-Pied-de-Port, I decided to stand up, walk out to the road, and take my first step. Before long, as I climbed the trail that led up and over the Pyrenees and across the border into Spain, I realized that I was feeling better. I met Julia, a *peregrina* from Munich, and we began talking, encouraging each other. Before the day was over, I would meet fellow travelers from other nations who would become traveling companions, mutual supporters, and fast friends as we all walked together toward our common destination.

It was a day of climbing—not just gaining altitude but also ascending past fears and uncertainties. As I leaned into the incline of the mountain pass, my calves burned and my tendons stretched. My backpack seemed to be dragging me backward. But by the end of the day, my companions and I were descending, looking forward to checking into the *albergue* in Roncesvalles, Spain, eating dinner, and resting for the next day's journey. We were fellow travelers, and we were on our way together. It felt right.

Each year hundreds of thousands of peregrinos walk some portion of the Camino de Santiago. There were 301,036 in 2017, and in 2018, the year of my walk, 327,378 completed their individual Camino.[1] In "Holy Years," when the Feast of St. James (July 25) falls on a Sunday, even more travelers make the journey. The day is easy for me to remember, because it also happens to be the date I founded my firm, Bernhardt Wealth Management.

Pilgrims on the Camino come from almost every part of the world, from a wide variety of ethnic, racial, political, and religious backgrounds. They are young, old, and everything in between. On the Camino, I met teenagers walking alone and also families walking together. I had one of my most meaningful conversations with a fellow peregrino in his seventies. Some people walk the route only once in a lifetime, and others return year after year.

Why do so many people from such widely varying backgrounds and ages feel drawn to walk the Camino de Santiago? I think the reason is something I heard over and over again as I traveled this path: "The Camino gives you what you need, not necessarily what you want." Having experienced the truth of this assertion, I can attest that this is a powerful motivation. Walking the Camino teaches lessons that you never looked for, that you didn't even know you needed. And the teaching is infinitely diverse, meticulously differentiated for each person who travels the path. Though all pilgrims walk the same Camino, each travels a unique road.

In fact, this is true in more than a metaphorical sense. The "Way of St. James" is really a network of main and secondary routes. The route I traveled, called the *Camino Francés* or French Way, begins in southern France at Saint-Jean-Pied-de-Port,

---

1   "The Tomb of the Apostle of the Cathedral of Santiago Goal of Pilgrimage of St. James," Oficina de Acogida al Peregrino, accessed on June 10, 2022, https://oficinadelperegrino.com/en/.

crosses the Pyrenees into northern Spain, and takes an inland route that passes through the major cities of Pamplona, Burgos, and León. This is the most popular route. Another route, the *Camino Primitivo*, or Original Way, begins in the city of Oviedo, near Spain's northern coast. The *Camino Portugués* begins in Lisbon, Portugal, and winds its way north along the coast. And there are many other subroutes, including the *Chemin de Paris* (Way of Paris) that trails south from the French capital before crossing into Spain and joining with the other routes.

What all of these routes have in common is their destination: the Cathedral of St. James ("Santiago" in Spanish) in the city of Santiago de Compostela, near the northwestern tip of Spain. Tradition holds that the cathedral contains the relics (remains) of St. James the Apostle. During the Middle Ages, making a pilgrimage was a way of exhibiting one's devotion and earning indulgences—much like religious merit badges. Along with the pilgrimage to Rome and the pilgrimage to Jerusalem, the Camino de Santiago became a principal route for religious devotees.

Of course much has changed since those earliest pilgrimages. In those days, one's pilgrimage began when one left home, whether from somewhere in the British Isles, northern France, Germany, or somewhere else in those parts of Europe loyal to the Roman Catholic Church. There was no such thing as a convenient form of transportation to a starting point like Saint-Jean-Pied-de-Port, Lisbon, or anywhere else. As soon as you started walking, you were on a pilgrimage, and it didn't end until you returned home—if you did. In those times, bandits often preyed on pilgrims traversing the lonely countryside, and a simple cold could develop into pneumonia or some other condition that, while easily treated with antibiotics now, often proved fatal then.

THE CAMINO IN LEGEND

The name of the city, Santiago de Compostela, and its cathedral arises from two sources: "Santiago" (St. James) and "Compostela," which is a Spanish place name compounded from the Latin words "campus stellae," or "field of stars." Legend has it that in 813 AD, a shepherd named Pelayo was drawn to a field near a place then called Libredon by a bright light or cluster of lights. Subsequently, the tomb of St. James was discovered in the hidden place where his followers had buried him centuries before, to avoid the desecration of his corpse by the minions of a pagan queen. The Roman Catholic bishop Theodomirus proclaimed the discovery of the holy remains, and the place became known as Santiago Compostela, honoring both the martyred apostle and the miracle of light that led to the recovery of his hidden burial place.

As a matter of fact, the many needs of vulnerable pilgrims in those earliest times led to the establishment of a network of overnight lodgings along the route, known as "hospitals" (note the same root as "hospitality"). Some towns along the route, founded as hospitals, still carry the name, such as Hospital de Órbigo, a small town just southeast of the city of León. Staffed by Catholic monks and under royal protection, the hospitals often tended to the needs of destitute, wounded, or ill pilgrims, giving rise to our modern concept of hospitals today.

Despite the many difficulties of travel in the Middle Ages, the Camino de Santiago became one of the most popular religious pilgrimages after its beginnings in the ninth century. One medieval legend stated that the Milky Way—which when viewed at night appears to lead roughly east to west and thus marks the general direction of the Camino—was created by the dust rising from the feet of the thousands of pilgrims who traversed the route. In fact, the popular Spanish name for the Milky Way is "El Camino de Santiago."

Of course, I didn't know all of this when I set out on that cool, cloudy day in Saint-Jean-Pied-de-Port. I only knew that this walk, this pilgrimage, was something I needed to do. I didn't know if my walk would be mostly solitary or mostly in the company of others. Either would have been fine with me; while I enjoy companionship, I'm also comfortable spending time with my own thoughts. I wasn't entirely sure how my body would respond to the demands of the trail, though I had spent time in conscientious physical preparation and also had methodically selected equipment—shoes, backpack, walking poles, and other items—best suited to my requirements and the demands of the journey. I didn't have particular expectations about the spiritual or emotional benefits I would reap from walking the Camino. I only knew that this pilgrimage was important; it was something I needed to do, even if I didn't fully understand the reasons at the time.

It didn't take long to learn, after I started walking with my fellow peregrinos, that each of us was traveling the Camino for as many reasons as individuals making the trip. While all of us had the same goal—to reach the Cathedral de Santiago de Compostela—every person I met on the route had a slightly different motivation, a slightly different way of thinking about the journey, a slightly different take on what they hoped to glean from the experience.

For many of the young people I met, especially those from Europe, walking the Camino was a rite of passage, a marker for moving from one phase of life to another—graduating secondary school or college, perhaps, or embarking on a new career. For some, simple curiosity was the motivating factor. They had heard of the Camino for many years, often from friends or family members, and wanted to see what it was all about.

Some of my fellow travelers would offer no reason other than the simple desire to reach the destination, to finish the course. Some, like me, couldn't really put words to what pulled them forward, other than the basic conviction that this journey meant something— it was a passage that urged us on for reasons we couldn't articulate. What gradually became clear to me was that all of us walking the path brought to the effort unique perspectives, motives, expectations, physical capabilities and challenges, and assumptions. Though each of us was walking the same route toward the same goal, each of us was also walking a different Camino.

It probably isn't surprising to learn that one reason people give for walking the Camino is to disconnect from the day-to-day busyness of modern life and to reconnect with something deeper and more contemplative: nature for some, spirituality for many, a personal goal or sense of purpose for most. In other words, a chance to step back from the relentless pace of career, family, and social obligations to just think, reflect, evaluate, and prioritize from the vantage point of the quiet space created by paying attention to the simple cadence of footsteps, heartbeat, and breath.

I am a wealth manager by trade, so naturally, as I made the journey, I thought a lot about what I do: the people served by my firm; the colleagues I work with; the way we counsel clients and how clients respond to that advice; the successes and failures I've experienced, both personally and professionally; and most importantly, the many relationships I've built over the years on the path of my work.

WHY DO PEOPLE WALK THE CAMINO DE SANTIAGO?

According to CaminoWays.com, a popular website for past or prospective peregrinos, people list seven main reasons for taking the pilgrimage:[2]

1. For a new challenge (28 percent)

2. For religious or spiritual reasons (28 percent)

3. To get away from it all/connect with nature (18 percent)

4. For health and exercise (11 percent)

5. To learn about other cultures (5 percent)

6. To meet new people (2 percent)

7. Something else (8 percent)

I suppose it would be easy for me, then, to reduce this book to a handbook of quick tips for investing success: "On this day, I walked with so-and-so, and she said this, and it reminded me of the time when the markets did this, and here's what you should do about that." I could add lots of sidebars with definitions of investment jargon and have a call

---

2 CaminoWays.com. "2019 Survey Results," www.caminoways. com/7-reasons-why-people-walk-camino.

to action at the end of each chapter. But that isn't the kind of story I want to tell. Instead I'm hoping to reach toward something larger, something more important than portfolio theory or investment psychology or whether you should focus on value or growth.

Sure, I couldn't help but relate many of my experiences on the Camino to my work. After all, the work we choose or are given is a good thing; it allows us to sustain ourselves and our families while contributing meaningfully to the lives of others. If I were an accountant—as I once was—I'm sure that my Camino would have led me to reflect on debits and credits, assets and liabilities, and how to know which is which. If I were an architect, my Camino would probably have induced thoughts about the importance of foundations, of using the right materials, of the ways in which people relate to the structures in which they live and work. If, like my father, I were a farmer and rancher, I would likely have spent time contemplating the terrain of northern Spain as it slowly unreeled before me: how the plants, animals, and people there joined together to sustain and nurture each other, and what that might reveal about my own relationships with places and people back home.

I am an investment counselor and wealth manager, however, and many of the lessons I took away from my pilgrimage are couched in terms of my professional experiences. But rather than trying to package the Camino as some sort of carbon-neutral, metaphysical continuing education seminar, I hope to convey the broader message that we are all fellow travelers. We are all on a journey. We all have blind spots, preconceived notions, vulnerabilities. We also have goals, dreams, priorities—people, things, ideas, and beliefs that are precious to us.

As we journey together, there is much we can learn from each other. At each stage of this pilgrimage called life, we can choose to be good and helpful traveling companions—or not. Everything depends on our ability to listen and be present: attending to each moment of the journey; heeding both the inner and outer voices; seeing the details of each moment; breathing, taking steps, and moving forward with purpose.

I gained insights on the Camino that will be fruitful for my work with clients and associates, and I want to share those with you. But more than that, I gained insights into the way I wish to inhabit this world, the way I want to walk my path, and the type of traveling companion I want to be for those making the pilgrimage along with me: clients, colleagues, friends, family, and even casual acquaintances.

In fact, my hopes for this book are perhaps best captured by the greeting one hears most often while walking the Way of St. James. Other peregrinos, people in the cities and towns along the route, those serving in the albergues and the small roadside stands offering fruit and water to pilgrims, and almost every other person you come in contact with will typically offer the salutation, "Buen camino!" The greeting simply means something like "Have a good journey," or maybe even "Happy trails." But over the course of the pilgrimage, this simple phrase comes to take on a much larger sense.

As one considers the many layers of meaning captured in the idea of this unique journey, "buen camino" acquires a deeper, richer connotation than simply saying "hi" or "have a nice day." It becomes a wish for every good thing; for a refreshed, clarified vision of one's life; for a broadened appreciation of this extraordinary world and our place in it. And perhaps most important of all, speaking and hearing "buen camino" reminds us that we are all fellow travelers: pilgrims who have come from many places but are all trying to reach a common destination.

This means we need to help each other. During today's walk, your feet may hurt or your legs may cramp, but I will walk beside you to encourage and help as best I can. Tomorrow, I may become thirsty and sunstruck, but you will give me a drink and help me find a shaded place to sit while I recover. That commitment to mutual caring is at the heart of "buen camino." It invokes the most precious good we can do for each other as human beings—to notice, to attend, to help. This book is about learning how to embody the deepest meaning of "buen camino" in all of life's circumstances.

So as you read, I hope that the story of my pilgrimage on the Camino de Santiago will lead you to reflect on your own journey—your Camino. You may never walk through Spain toward the Cathedral de Santiago de Compostela, but you are a peregrino—a pilgrim—all the same. I hope some of the thoughts and impressions I share can benefit you in ways both tangible and intangible. I hope I can help you learn to be careful in the places where the path becomes harder to see, so that you don't waste time walking in the wrong direction. I hope I can encourage you to raise your eyes from the road beneath your feet now and then, so you can notice the amazing sights along the way.

And as you walk, you can take comfort in remembering that the Camino will give you what you need.

Buen camino!

CHAPTER 1

"March Forth!"

I have a theory that everybody has at least one person in their life who is a "thought of you" sender. You are probably already thinking of that person in your circle: maybe your mom, a cousin, a friend at work, or somebody else who consistently sends email attachments, social media messages, or some other transmission accompanied by words like, "Saw this and thought of you." It could be a news article, a meme, an image, the title of a book, or almost anything. The point is that for the "thought of you" sender, something about that particular bit of information brought you to their mind. And of course, in these days of email, tagging on Facebook and Instagram, and DM-ing on Twitter, it's easier than ever. Personally, I haven't decided if that's a good thing or a bad thing.

In my life, my sister Gloria is my "thought of you" sender. She is in the habit of sending voicemails and emails or dropping into conversations various topics or pieces of information that she associates with me in some way. Sometime in 2011, the Camino de Santiago came to her attention, and it found its way to my attention because Gloria thought of me.

INSPIRATION IN VERSE

One of the first things I remember my sister Gloria sending me was a poem titled "March Fourth," by master swimmer Ande Rasmussen.[3] Through the years, I have reread the poem many times, both because of its personal significance for me and because I think it is a really fine poem.

March Fourth

We all love Christmas. Halloween is scary sweet.
I'm thankful for Thanksgiving, Boy how we eat!
Then there's our birthday, which is really fun.
New Year's Eve is festive but we're a little tired
come January One.

Easter is delightful! Fourth of July fireworks are
great!
There's St. Patrick's, Presidents, Valentines,
Veterans, Labor,
Columbus, Flag, Fathers, Mothers, Martin Luther
King,...
How do we keep track of all of these darn dates?

When I look at my one-year calendar,
March Fourth is my favorite day.
Nothing special happened in history.
It's just what that day has to say!

When you have problems, March Forth!
When things don't work out, March Forth!

---

3   Ande Rasmussen, "March Fourth," (1999), quoted in *Inspirations for Songwriters.*

When bad things happen, March Forth!
When you lose, March Forth!

When anything can happen, March Forth says it all.
If something does happen,
Get up, brush off, and March Forth,
Because we're all bound to fall.

—Ande Rasmussen

Call of the Way

Prior to my sister's thoughtful encouragement, I had taken an interest in hiking. I had participated in the Sierra Club's One Day Hike between Washington, DC and Harper's Ferry, West Virginia. The organization offers both a fifty-kilometer and a hundred-kilometer hike, and I had done the 50K three times. I also had hiked to the bottom of the Grand Canyon and back up again after spending a few nights at Phantom Ranch, and it was one of the best experiences of my life. So I guess it's not surprising that when my sister came across information about the Camino, it made her think of her brother and his penchant for walking long distances in open country.

Not long after Gloria put the idea in my mind, it began to take root. She told me about *The Way*, a movie about the Camino starring Martin Sheen and directed by his son, Emilio Estevez. I bought a copy and watched it, and I also started buying and reading books about the Camino. The more I learned about this pilgrimage, the more I began to imagine myself participating. Before long, I realized that walking the French Way, from Saint-Jean-Pied-de-Port to the Cathedral de Santiago de

Compostela, was on my bucket list, for better or worse. At the end of 2016, I made the commitment to myself that I would walk the Camino in 2018. It had gone from something my sister thought of to something I had firmly purposed to do.

In fact, as I think about it, the reason I settled on 2018 as the year of my Camino also had to do with a goal of mine. I have three sisters and several nieces and nephews. A few years back, I made it my aim that each time one of them graduated from high school, I would invite them to spend ten weeks of the summer with me at my home in the Washington, DC area. That's a pretty big time commitment, but it's important to me to cultivate meaningful relationships with them and provide an opportunity for them to see and appreciate the many sites so central to our nation's history and character.

Looking ahead, I knew that the summer of 2017 would be devoted to my twin nieces from Texas, and that the next time a niece would be graduating would be in 2019. So the summer of 2018 was free of commitments; my walk through Spain would have to take place then. It was settled as an official, honest-to-goodness goal.

The Goal of Being and Becoming

I assume everyone is different when it comes to goal setting. I know some people who regard it as more than a good idea. Everything important in their lives, be it their business, family, or some aspect of personal improvement, is framed in terms of a goal. And judging by the sheer number of self-help and success coaching books in libraries and bookstores, there must be many folks like this. There are dozens of books that can take you from A to Z in goal setting, breaking it all down into microsteps to unlock the transformative power of goal setting for your life and career.

I'm certainly not opposed to such books or the whole result-oriented concept informing the mini-industry that has grown around setting and achieving goals. I've read many of those books in my career. I believe we should all have meaningful aims in life, and we should be willing to work to achieve them. At my wealth management firm, in order to assist clients in accomplishing what is important in their lives, we ask them to list the goals that take time, money, and planning to achieve. But for me, I find that a goal needs to be something I want to become, rather than something I want to achieve or accomplish. It's more about an understanding to be gained, a personal quality to be strengthened, a friendship to be enhanced.

I think this is why walking the Camino became so important to me. Perhaps through my experiences hiking the Grand Canyon and other long-distance treks, I had begun to learn that such experiences could teach me something about myself and others that I might not be able to learn any other way. Over the years, I have learned to pay attention to that inner voice.

Indeed, listening to that quiet, internal prompt is the reason I live and work where I do. When I was a student at a small college in northwest Nebraska, just a few miles down the road from where I grew up, something deep inside whispered that I needed to be in Washington, DC. I applied for an internship in the office of my US representative—and was turned down. So the next summer, after I applied again, I mounted a public relations campaign. I enlisted about fifty local businesspeople, student leaders, professors, high school teachers, and even the president of my college to write letters to Congresswoman Virginia Smith, asking her to consider my application.

I don't know if she was persuaded by the sincerity of the letters or if her staff got sick of handling all the extra mail, but one day I got a phone call from her office, telling me I could knock it off with the letters; I had the internship. After arriving in Washington, DC in time for President Reagan's inauguration, I would subsequently have the opportunity to work for Congresswoman Smith and then for the US Senate Finance Committee, chaired by Senator Bob Dole. I went on to complete my college education at the University of Virginia and entered the workforce full-time, originally as a CPA for PricewaterhouseCoopers. I have lived in the DC area ever since, and I can't imagine living anywhere else while I am still working.

In the same way that my "inner guide" had led me from northwest Nebraska to DC all those years ago, I now felt it leading me to a walk in Spain. In fact, there was something inherently "inner" about the pull of the Camino; maybe that's why it clicked with me so strongly. As I continued to read about and research the pilgrimage and its history, I kept coming across advice like this, from the introduction to John Brierley's guidebook, *A Pilgrim's Guide to the Camino de Santiago*,[4] which I carried with me on my walk:

> What inspired me to write another guidebook was the almost universal absence of any reference, let alone way-marks, to the *inner* path...A core question arises: What turns a walking holiday into pilgrimage? When you receive an answer, you may find a fundamental change in how you

---

4   John Brierley, *A Pilgrim's Guide to the Camino de Santiago: St. Jean Roncesvalles Santiago* (Forres, Scotland: Findhorn, 2009).

approach the journey—from intention down to what you put in your backpack…You will know when something rings true for you; learn to trust that resonance…

When I read these words, I knew exactly what Brierley meant; the Camino de Santiago was already beginning to resonate within me. My inner guide was endorsing the journey. It became more than a goal; it became a purpose—a journey toward fulfillment.

I created an album on Facebook and began recording images and thoughts about the Camino and my preparation for it. In some ways, I began to realize that my Camino had begun years before when I hiked the C&O Canal towpath on the Sierra Club's One Day Hike, and later when I felt the immense solitude enveloping me on my hike to the bottom of the Grand Canyon. It had probably begun even earlier, when as a high school graduate, I felt pulled to the great city beside the Potomac River where I now live. In fact, as I reflected on it, it seemed that everything that had happened to me, from growing up on a farm outside Hay Springs, Nebraska, to leaving my work as a CPA to enter the financial services industry had in some way placed my feet on the path that was leading me toward the Cathedral de Santiago de Compostela.

On February 18, 2018, about five months before I would leave for France to begin my Camino, I wrote this in my Facebook album:

Today I walked ten miles in some new shoes. They were fine except for how one toe felt…I found this photo on the web. It represents a view from the Camino as one would go through the Pyrenees. I am looking forward to seeing what I will see when I begin my pilgrimage.

Accompanying my text was an image taken from the trail leading over the Pyrenees from southern France into northern Spain. It depicts a series of green hills, separated by steep mist-filled valleys, receding into the distance beneath a cloudy sky. I recall vividly when, on the first day of my walk, I paused on the trail to take my own picture of this very same scene.

Posting a photo of where I was going helped me to see my goal even before I got there. It made it real in my mind. This is just one more way, I now realize, that I was beginning my walk, even before I boarded my flight to Paris. By visualizing my destination, I was making progress toward arriving there. Perceiving my goal in this way may have actually been the most important preparation that I did.

A view from the trail as I crossed the Pyrenees on July 20, 2018.

As you might imagine, my conception of my goal changed as I continued my preparation, and even as I walked the Camino in

Spain. On July 26, 2018, as I was in the midst of my pilgrimage, I wrote this on my Facebook page:

> I had a great day on the Camino even though it was hot and the distance was long. In fact, I walked 18.8 miles from Los Arcos to Logroño...I want to comment on a question Rob from the Netherlands asked me yesterday. It is a good question and a question most pilgrims ask each other: "What is your goal?" I have met some pilgrims who are dealing with loss and others who are searching for purpose. Their goal may very well be dealing with those issues.
>
> In my case, this is something I have wanted to do for many years. And I think Rob expected me to say my goal is to get to Santiago de Compostela or something very tangible. I told him that is not my goal because I believe the Camino will continue to influence me for weeks, months, or years after I get home. My goal is to be present and open to all possibilities. I don't think the Camino ends.
>
> It makes me think about discussions we have with clients about their goals. Retirement is always one of them and should be. I certainly want to retire someday or at least have a goal to make work optional. Retirement, in this case, is represented by Santiago. You reach Santiago—now what? The really big goals are about legacy and purpose. So I want to always be open to legacy and purpose on this trip and for years to come.

These remarks on my Facebook page get at one of the first things I said about goals: that for me, a goal tends to be more about something I want to *be* rather than something I want to do. Yes, walking the Camino was an action—it was something I did. But the reason I did it wasn't just to reach Santiago de Compostela. I did it to learn, to grow—to experience transformation.

The problem I have with "doing" goals is that by pursuing them, you often end up like many of our clients planning for retirement. You achieve your goal, and then you have to ask yourself, "Now what?" By contrast, "being" goals bring with them their own justification. When I feel myself growing, I don't have to wonder, "Now what?" I am already reaping the understanding and benefits of my journey toward the goal.

This also reminds me that "being" goals are less susceptible to derailment by circumstances. If my goal is simply to walk to Santiago de Compostela—to be able to say that I got there successfully—my sense of completion is subject to a host of potential events over which I have no control. I could fall and break a leg (which I almost did, as I'll explain later). Political or military events or a pandemic could prevent me from finishing my walk. I could get sick and be unable to continue. There could be an earthquake or a flood.

But if my goal is to remain present in the moment and open to all possibilities, then there is really nothing that can get between me and my ultimate aim. Remember, the Camino gives you what you need, not necessarily what you want. The trick, then, is not to wish you had something else, but rather to find the benefit, the lesson, the opportunity for growth in what you have. When that is your goal, you never have to ask, "Now what?"

My long experience with clients at our firm has shown me that most have thought through at least some of the larger questions of what they want their lives to stand for. They have already dealt with the "now what?" I doubt that a single one of our clients, when asked about their goals for their financial lives or their desired outcomes from our planning services, would say, "I want to die as rich as possible." For the vast majority, their larger goals have something to do with legacy, their ongoing impact on the lives of other people and important causes, an impact that they aspire to perpetuate even beyond their lifetimes.

In helping clients plan strategies and tactics for meeting those transformative goals, we become fellow travelers. We provide the assistance, tools, and insights they need to release the day-to-day management of accounts, documents, and assets to us, and instead spend their creative energies casting a vision for something that will go on after their departure.

As my fellow traveler Rob did for me on the Camino, we can ask them, "What is your goal?" and then assist them in not only clarifying the answer, but also making it an unfolding reality. We are driven to help busy, high-achieving people focus on creating their legacy and realizing their purpose by reassuring them that we are monitoring the financial operations. When we can do that for them, walk alongside and help them answer the question, "What is your goal?", we are providing one of the most valuable types of companionship that people can offer each other. It's our opportunity to live the reality of "buen camino."

Planning for a goal implies preparation, and my journey as a peregrino was no different in that respect. But what sort of preparation should one make for a goal that really has no expiration date? Obviously I needed to train myself physically for the walk, but what about the inner preparation that would enable me to reach my true goal?

In the travel guide I carried, John Brierley writes of this inner preparation: "Take time to prepare a purpose for this pilgrimage... Start from the basis that you are essentially a spiritual being on a human journey, not a human being on a spiritual one. We came to learn some lesson, and this pilgrimage affords an opportunity to find out what that is..."

I learned during my preparation phase that inner and outer preparation are more closely related than we often realize. It's easy to observe what someone is *doing* to get ready, but it's harder to perceive what that doing is making them *become*. Still, that relationship is there, all the same: what we do affects who we are, and vice versa.

The inner journey—and the learning that goes along with it—is the topic for discussion in the next chapter.

For Reflection

- If you have goals that take time, money, and planning to achieve, what are they?

- Are you making progress toward your goals?

- What do you want your legacy to be?

Scan to see a color image of the photo in this chapter.

CHAPTER 2

The Inner Journey

Most of us have heard some variation of the maxim, "The will to win is less important than the will to prepare to win." Those who played any sort of organized sport, especially in high school or college, have probably heard it dozens of times from various coaches. It has been attributed to Vince Lombardi, Bobby Knight, Joe Paterno, and probably several others.

As it turns out, the originator of the quote is likely Fielding Yost, who coached the Michigan Wolverines football team from 1901 to 1926. Over his lifetime, he compiled an impressive 198-35-12 record as a collegiate head coach, notching six national championships and ten Big 10 conference titles. Yost also coached at Nebraska during the 1898 season, which is probably my favorite thing about him, as those who know me also know that I'm a diehard Nebraska football fan.

It's easy to understand how Yost's maxim became so well known; it appeals strongly to our sense of logic and experience. We have all known, either through personal involvement or close acquaintance, how much more enjoyable it is to win than to lose. But we also understand intuitively that winning consistently becomes much more likely when we make the right kind of preparation for the contest. From clinching the tournament with your basketball team to acing your history midterm, success is typically dictated by the quality of your preparation. When you're grinding out that last wind-sprint at practice or reviewing one more chapter in your textbook, you're voting for the truth of Coach Yost's assertion that those who are dedicated to the right preparation will generally perform better than those who aren't.

But what about preparing for an undertaking where the end point is harder to define? As I contemplated the goal I had set for myself to complete the Camino de Santiago, I soon understood that this was about far more than simply walking a route and reaching a finish line. I realized I hoped for much more as a result of achieving this goal. As I mentioned in the last chapter, I realized that I wanted something bigger—something defined more by transformation than completion. Certainly I would need to prepare physically. I would also require material preparation to make good decisions about what to bring with me. But there was unquestionably a spiritual and emotional dimension to my preparation for the Camino that would be just as important.

When you think about it, this is true of most major endeavors in life. There is almost always an inner and an outer aspect to proper preparation. The two are intimately connected in our lives. As John Brierley alluded in my travel guide, our spiritual and physical journeys are going on simultaneously, affecting and being affected by each other at every moment.

For example, when we counsel clients who are approaching retirement, we don't just talk about money, assets, and bank accounts—the outer aspects. We also discuss the many emotional challenges that arise for those who will soon be finding themselves, after a lifetime of diligent work and the challenges that go with it, with much more time on their hands. We want these clients to prepare themselves for a very different day-to-day world. In a spiritual sense, we are asking them to come to grips with who they understand themselves to be.

After decades of defining themselves largely in terms of what they accomplish at the office, how will they recognize the real self that lies beneath all the activity? What is really important to them? What are the causes and relationships most central to their self-identity—elements of themselves that will live on after their eulogies? Retirement preparation that doesn't take these crucial inner elements into account is unlikely to enjoy long-term success. We know this about our clients because we know how true it is in our own lives. In fact, one of the twenty-six guiding principles at our firm—the code that we refer to as "The Bernhardt Way"—is that we take the same care of our clients that we would want someone to take for our loved ones: "Care Like It's Your Family."

With family, you don't worry only about the outer journey, do you? When I was a little boy, my parents didn't just make sure I was clothed and fed. They also invested in my mind and heart, because they wanted to equip me for the inner journey of life. If you are raising children, you completely understand this. You aspire for your children to not only be cared for financially but also nourished emotionally, intellectually, and spiritually. You don't want them just to survive; you want them to develop into mature, self-assured, and capable adults. We aspire to this same level of caring for our clients.

This is why, as I mentioned before, we place immense importance on becoming valued partners on our clients' life journeys. Among other things, we want them to be able to rely on us to facilitate the daily management of their financial affairs (the outer journey), which affords them the freedom to spend their mental and emotional energies on building and solidifying their legacies (the inner journey). We want to give them the luxury of completing the sort of emotional, intellectual, and spiritual preparation for themselves and their loved ones that leads to the deepest, most meaningful kind of success.

A Pilgrim's Guide

As I began preparing myself for the Camino de Santiago, I started reading everything I could find about the pilgrimage, its history, and the advice and reflections of those who had made the journey. As you can probably imagine, there is an abundance of travel guides available to aid those walking the Camino. You can read books that tell you what to pack (and what to avoid packing), books with all kinds of maps, and books with a deeply spiritual focus. There are guidebooks for every main route, and there are even guidebooks especially designed for older folks who want to make the pilgrimage.

In the months leading up to my departure for Spain, I read John Brierley's travel guide, absorbing his advice, as I noted in Chapter 1. Brierley devotes a significant portion of his introduction to the sort of inner preparation I've been talking about. In helping the prospective peregrino to grapple with the question "why am I doing this," Brierley writes:

A majority of those setting out on the Camino de Santiago give a religious or spiritual reason for going, yet few appear to undertake any conscious inner preparation for the journey. It is so easy to allow the demands of our secular life to rob us of time for such preparation...And how, in this busy, secular world of ours, do we prepare for such a journey? A useful guideline is to spend *at least* as much time on inner preparation as on general logistics [emphasis mine]. This way we balance the inner and outer realities and give equal account to both...

Brierley's comments immediately made sense to me. I knew that I wanted to approach my Camino as much more than simply a course with a finish line at the end. I wanted to be keenly aware of the inner journey, allowing it to shape and guide the outer journey, recognizing that the two are inextricably linked.

A fellow pilgrim, Joyce Rupp, makes this link very clear in her book, *Walk in a Relaxed Manner: Life Lessons from the Camino.*[5] Rupp, seventy-seven, is a Servite sister in the Roman Catholic Church who walked the Camino in 2003. She walked the French Way, the same route I took, with her friend, Father Tom Pfeffer, a priest from her hometown of Des Moines, Iowa. In her book, she discusses the process of weighing the items that she would put in her backpack in order to make decisions about the things that were most necessary to bring and those that could be left behind. One of the universal rules in every guidebook is the importance of minimizing the weight of your backpack; the

5   Joyce Rupp, *Walk in a Relaxed Manner: Life Lessons from the Camino* (Ossining, New York: Orbis Books, 2005).

consensus is that you shouldn't try to carry more than about twenty pounds, and it's better if you can get by with less. Rupp soon learned that this can create some tough dilemmas.

She writes, "I thought I had a fairly simple lifestyle. I quickly found out this idea was a giant illusion. As the stack of items I hoped to take kept getting reduced, it turned out that I really had a lot of *stuff*...Finally, after several weeks of annoyingly weighing every item, my backpack of seventeen pounds was ready." A few paragraphs later, she tells the story of a day on the Camino when she made a decision that to her—and to most of us—would seem pretty inconsequential. She added a tomato, freshly plucked from the vine and given to her by an old Spanish gardener. She accepted the tomato gratefully and, without much thought, she put it in the top flap pocket of her backpack. Only later, after walking much of the day with an irritating tension in her neck, did she realize that the weight of the tomato, added to the top of her backpack, was enough to cause a problem. "Imagine," she writes, "a single tomato causing all that discomfort!"

Rupp's comments point to one of the more obvious linkages between inner and outer preparation: in carefully evaluating what I needed to bring, it soon became obvious to me that most of us carry a lot of extra weight in our backpacks. Now, this isn't headed for a critique of the consumer-driven culture that constantly nags us about all the stuff we need in order to live fulfilled lives, though that is certainly a topic we all need to grapple with. Beyond that, it occurred to me that we carry a lot of unnecessary mental and emotional weight around with us all the time: fretful thoughts about things that might happen; anxiety about what others think of us; and most of all, worry about things that we can't control. I'll be the first to admit that I'm not exactly a Zen master; I spend my own fair share of time stewing about one thing or another, and most of the time it doesn't accomplish much of anything. But as I prepared myself inwardly for my Camino, I began to reflect on all of that extra mental and emotional weight, and how I might go about eliminating it.

It's much the same in the world of finance. One of my favorite bits of Wall Street wisdom comes from the great Nobel Prize-winning economist Paul Samuelson, who said, "The stock market has predicted nine of the last five recessions." In other words, the financial markets, like most of us, have a tendency to worry about things that don't actually come to pass. In fact, as we work with clients, we typically advise them that one of the principles of successful investing is the ability to tune out the noise created by the financial media: dire headlines, bold predictions, pitches from the financial gurus du jour. All of that stuff is calculated to generate clicks, likes, follows, and above all, advertising revenue for the newspapers, magazines, and websites that produce the daily barrage of information minus the necessary context. Many of my colleagues and I say, "You cannot expect to consistently improve your outcomes by reacting to breaking news." The report goes on to advise against basing any investment program on reacting to or trying to anticipate the unexpected, which is beyond anyone's control or ability. Instead you should focus on things you can actually do something about.

So as I went about my inner preparation for the Camino de Santiago, I resolved to get rid of as much excess baggage as possible. My aim was to focus my attention on the present moment: to be *here*, *now*, instead of allowing my mind to wander off, either to some past event that couldn't be changed, or to some uncertain future concern that may never occur. *Being present* became my mantra. I wanted to notice each moment as I lived it. After all, I would never have the chance to live that moment again. As I said to my hiking partner Rob from the Netherlands, I wanted "to be present and open to all possibilities."

In truth, I'm still working on this, as I expect I always will be.

THE CROSS AND THE SCALLOP

The Cross of St. James originated in the twelfth century as the emblem of the Order of Santiago, formed as a military order for the protection of pilgrims traveling the Camino de Santiago.

A Santiago Cross in my hand.

In heraldic uses, the cross is often topped with what is called an "escallop," which is basically a Mediterranean scallop shell. Like the Cross of St. James, the scallop is often used as a symbol for the pilgrimage of the Camino de Santiago. Most peregrinos have a scallop shell—often with a red Cross of Saint James painted on it—attached to their backpacks. Some peregrinos even paint their country's flag or some other image that is significant for them on their scallop shell. Many road markers along the way feature a scallop, sometimes highly stylized.

The scallop is associated with the Camino de Santiago because of some of the legends that have grown up around the pilgrimage over the centuries.

The Scallop shell I placed on my backpack.

One such legend has it that as St. James's followers were bringing his body to Spain for burial, a storm at sea washed his corpse overboard. However, days later, the undamaged body washed ashore, covered in scallop shells.

A waymarker with a stylized symbol of the scallop shell.

Another version tells of a wedding taking place on the shore near where the ship carrying St. James's body would land. The groom was mounted on a horse, and the sight of the approaching ship spooked the animal, which bolted into the ocean. The groom fell off his horse and drowned but was then miraculously drawn from the water alive and covered in scallop shells.

Over the centuries, the scallop has become inextricably tied to the Camino de Santiago, and one reason may be that the ancient pilgrims were in the habit of carrying such a shell to use as a lightweight bowl for eating and drinking. It is also said that the converging ridges on the shell symbolize the many paths taken by pilgrims as they converge on the Cathedral de Santiago de Compostela.

Preparation Inside and Out

On August 8, 2018, I was slightly past the halfway point of my Camino, leaving the city of León, just over three hundred kilometers from the Cathedral de Santiago de Compostela. León is a popular starting point for many peregrinos, since it is still far enough from Santiago de Compostela to fulfill the minimum distance requirement for receiving a certificate of completion for the pilgrimage. (The minimum distance for walking is one hundred kilometers; for bicycle riders it is two hundred kilometers.) That day, I wrote these words on my Facebook page:

> As I was walking out of León I was approaching a pilgrim. I started a conversation and learned her name was Paula (not sure if she spells it this way) and that she was from Italy. She just started her Camino today from León. It turns out that she did no preparation and only bought her gear days ago when she decided to do the Camino. Internally, I was grimacing and concerned for her. But I tried to encourage her and told her not to walk someone else's Camino but to walk her pace and appreciate each moment. Unfortunately, she mentioned she was getting a blister, and I told her to address it quickly. I helped as much as I could and then stopped for breakfast. I ran into her later at another café, and she had other blisters already. I wished her the best, told her to take care of herself, and kept going. As I left, I said a little prayer for her. I truly hope she makes it to Santiago and has a good Camino.

This emphasized to me the importance of planning. In my case, I did a reasonable amount of walking almost every weekend in 2018. And even then, I was concerned I did not walk enough. I also tried seven or eight pairs of trail running shoes before I settled on the shoes I have. If I had done no training, and if I had come to Spain with the first pair of shoes I tried, I can only imagine the number of blisters I would have and the pain I would be in.

This is really a lesson on the importance of planning, whether it is to walk the Camino, plan for retirement, plan for college education, plan for an exit from a business, or anything else.

A little later, I'll explain in greater detail about how much importance I placed on having the right shoes and why I tried so many different pairs before settling on the shoes that would carry me along the Camino de Santiago. But for now, I'll just say that I spent a considerable amount of time on outer preparation as well. As I look back on my Facebook entries for the days preceding my departure for the Camino, many are dedicated to the training walks I took, mostly along the C&O Canal that runs along the Potomac River from Washington, DC to Cumberland, Maryland.

These preparatory hikes were important for obvious reasons. I needed to learn how my body responded to walking long distances, sometimes on consecutive days. Starting in April, I began training hikes with a loaded backpack. I even managed to get in a 7.5-mile and a 9.28-mile hike while I was attending a business conference in Colorado Springs. In early May, based on my reading about the Camino and my research in various travel guides and online sources, I purchased the backpack, waterproof poncho, and trekking poles that I would use in Spain. On the long weekend of May 26–28, 2018, I walked three consecutive days, logging almost forty-three miles. It was important to me to make sure that I was ready, inside and out, for the pilgrimage that I would make in July and August.

But even as I was training my body and acquiring the necessary equipment, I was also practicing the art of being present that was so vital to my inner training. As I look back on my Facebook entries during the period from mid-February 2018 until my final training hike on July 8, I'm pleased to see the pictures that I took along the way: the places, people, and things I noticed. I made comments on the weather, the plants and wildlife I saw, and the people who walked the trail with me.

Some of them shared stories I found meaningful, such as Dr. Bob, a retiree in the DC area who served as a Boy Scout leader for more than twenty years. He was preparing to complete the Appalachian Trail that summer, after which he intended to hike the Pacific Coast Trail in 2019 and the Continental Divide Trail in 2020: the Triple Crown of US hiking, a total of 5,549 miles. He was a great trail companion and a world-class hiker.

On my April 28 hike, I was on the trail the same day as competitors in the two-day American Odyssey Relay race, which begins in Gettysburg, Pennsylvania, and ends in Washington, DC. One of the runners was carrying an American flag over his shoulder as he jogged along; I thought that was really neat.

On the three-day weekend at the end of May, I happened to be walking past a group of kids fishing in the C&O Canal when one of them hooked a fish. The man who was supervising the group helped him reel it in, and it was fun to see how excited the boy and his friends were about snagging that three-pound channel catfish.

If I had walked all those miles on the C&O Canal focused solely on preparing physically—if I had not embraced the inner, spiritual preparation that called me to be present in each moment—I would have missed all these important opportunities for awareness. I would have failed to embrace my best chance for the type of transformation I hoped to gain from my pilgrimage. I might have walked the Camino, but I would have missed out on letting the Camino walk me.

Joyce Rupp writes, "The Camino forces the pilgrim into the present moment. There's really nowhere else to go. The longer one is on the Camino, the greater the possibility of developing oneness with the road and with life." That oneness, that absorbing awareness of the importance of *now*, was what I was seeking. I have come to believe that it may be the most important thing anyone can seek. And more than anything, I wanted to be ready to find it when the opportunity came.

Of course all the preparation in the world accomplishes nothing unless you really sign on the dotted line. There comes a time when all the planning, all the forethought, all the research and prioritizing bring you to the moment of go or no-go, the point of no return.

Eventually you have to commit. And that's the next part of my story.

For Reflection

- What is your attitude toward planning ahead? Do you consider yourself a planner, or are you more the "wing it" type?

- If your house was burning and you had to grab only one thing (assuming all your family members and pets were already safe), what would it be?

Scan to see a color image of the photos in this chapter.

CHAPTER 3

Booking the Ticket

Soon after I made my decision to walk the Camino de Santiago, I began telling friends and family about it, not to boast about my intentions, but to share what was becoming meaningful to me.

One of my friends told me in a sort of teasing way that my journey to Spain wouldn't be official until I had booked my airline ticket. And so, on April 22, 2018, I wrote these words on my Facebook page, next to a superimposed image of Earth with the flight path from Dulles International Airport to Paris, France:

I am posting this image out of respect to my friend, Pete. He joked and said my trip wasn't official until I booked my flight. Of course, I jokingly argued that it was official ever since 2016 when I told my sister the twins had to come last summer. In honor of Pete, I am announcing that the flight has been booked. I depart from Washington Dulles on July 17th and fly to Paris. I return to Dulles from Madrid in time for Nebraska's first football game of the 2018 season. Obviously, I have my priorities established. Thanks, Pete!

Commitment to Others and Ourselves

I should probably explain a bit about my friend, Pete, and his importance to my Camino journey. Pete Schwartz is a friend, a Master Chair (a member who coaches others) of Vistage, a business leadership group to which I belong, and a fellow peregrino who walked his Camino in 2015.

A few years earlier over breakfast, we had learned that we both wanted to walk the Camino. When Pete committed to his Camino in 2015, I accompanied him on some of his training walks. While he was completing his journey, he made daily posts on a blog. I read his entries and tracked his progress in my guidebook. I also posted a comment every day to his blog. When he returned, he said my comments were a huge encouragement to him on his journey. I really didn't understand exactly what he meant until I walked my own Camino. The comments, likes, loves, and other social media feedback that I received really did keep me motivated and encouraged. The day after I returned from my Camino, I met Pete for dinner. I considered him my Camino mentor, since he was the only person I knew who had completed the journey.

At some point in our lives, we all need someone like my friend Pete who can cheerfully encourage us to honor our commitments. I'm not saying that I wouldn't have booked the ticket without Pete's playful inspiration; after all, by that time I had been taking long training hikes for almost three months. In fact, the day I posted my tongue-in-cheek tribute to Pete on Facebook, I had hiked 11.22 miles on the C&O Canal, from Swains Lock to Violettes Lock. But it's a gift to have people in your life with whom you can share your goals, and who you can also depend on to help you stay on track to meet your goals. It's a good thing to surround yourself with a culture of commitment.

Me with my friend, fellow peregrino, and Camino mentor Pete Schwartz.

That's also one of the great things about where I work. We have built a team of individuals who are fundamentally committed to the well-being of our clients. That commitment is crystallized in the first tenet of what we call The Bernhardt Way: "Put clients first, always." We are utterly serious about honoring the trust our clients place in us when they hire us for their investment and wealth management planning. We refuse to permit conflicts of interest or personal biases to impact the services we provide. Along with the rest of my team, I believe sincerely that this is the best and only way we can be helpful to those who entrust to us their financial well-being.

Similarly, we ask for commitment from our clients. We spend a generous amount of time getting to know them in a much deeper way than simply learning about their financial affairs. We want to know what is really important to them, what they hope to accomplish, and what sort of legacy they would like to leave behind. Only then, after we have a clear picture in mind of who they really are, do we help them develop a financial plan and strategy for realizing their most important goals.

Sticking to that long-term plan also requires commitment on the client's part. Too often investors are swayed by the siren song of a "sure thing" or headline-inspired fears of an imminent market downturn. These emotional impulses derail most investors, pulling them off the strategic route to their goals and sending them on side trails that typically result in lost opportunities and wasted time. What we ask from our clients, instead, is the commitment to remain disciplined, to be guided by evidence-based research, and to remain focused on their long-term goals and priorities. Because we are committed to them and their welfare, we want them to be equally committed to the strategies that will take them where they want to go. In this sense, commitment is very much a two-way street.

This points to an essential aspect of commitment, and certainly one that was important to me as I walked the Camino de Santiago: commitment functions best in community. Our firm has a culture of commitment among its members, and in turn we invite our clients to become part of that culture. One of the biggest advantages of living in a community with a culture of commitment is the way that it calls forth mutual accountability. When you are in community with others who share your commitment, you don't want to disappoint each other. This calls forth the best in everyone.

As I began my walk from Saint-Jean-Pied-de-Port, the importance of a community of commitment became clear. When I took those first few steps—wondering if I would be able to continue—I was soon joined by Julia from Munich and, later that day, by Philipp, Astrid, and Tanja from Austria, as well as Szandra and Petra from Hungary. Having companions for the trail who shared my commitment to reaching the destination was, especially on that first day, one of the best things that could have happened. Here is my Facebook entry for that first day of walking on July 20, 2019:

Wow. Darn Tough. Wow. I didn't get much sleep last night. The room was stuffy and warm. Nevertheless, I left Saint-Jean-Pied-de-Port at 7:20 a.m., crossed the Pyrenees, and walked to Roncesvalles in Spain. It took nine hours and nineteen minutes to walk 16.24 miles door-to-door, and included an elevation gain of 4,554 feet. Like I said, it was tough, but it was a really great day. Much of the day you could hardly see twenty feet in front of you, which meant one had to be careful not to miss the trail.

I actually prayed for a sunny day before I left America, but I am glad my prayer was not answered. The cooler weather made it better if you consider tough better. But I am really grateful for this day.

I am also grateful for my hiking partner, Julia from Munich. She really was the perfect partner. I think we encouraged each other in ways few others could have. I am also thankful for others I hiked with for portions of the hike and had dinner with later.

Dinner in Roncesvalles with my new friends from the Fellowship. From left to right: Philipp, Tanja, Astrid, Julia, Petra, and Szandra.

As I look back on my life, I realize that I was always surrounded by a culture of commitment to caring for others. One of the most vivid memories of my young life is from a day when I was eight years old, riding with my dad in his pickup along a narrow Nebraska farm road on a hot summer evening. An old, battered pickup was coming toward us, and because the road was narrow, my dad slowed and pulled over to allow the other vehicle to pass.

But it didn't pass. Instead, it stopped, and the driver, a tired-looking Native American with a wind- and sun-creased face, leaned out his window. "I cut cedar posts for the farms and ranches around here," he told my dad, "but my chainsaw is busted. If you can give me a little money to fix it, I'll give you a good deal on cedar posts, anytime you need them."

Now, my family, like many rural families in that part of the country, was not wealthy. Dad worked hard on the farm; he was not some corporate farmer in a late-model, air-conditioned pickup who could afford to do "windshield farming," driving from field to field telling hired hands what to do. My mom took care of us kids, worked in the garden, kept the house, and did whatever else it took to keep things running. I knew for a fact that if my dad had any cash in his wallet, it wouldn't be much.

But he thought for a few seconds, nodded, and leaned over to pull his wallet from his hip pocket. He handed some bills to the man, who thanked him before we both drove on.

Even today, when I think about that chance encounter on a dirt road in northwest Nebraska, I'm astounded all over again. My dad thought more about what that other guy needed than about himself. Something clicked in my eight-year-old mind that day: caring for others was what my life was supposed to be about. Like my mom and dad, I wanted to be a person who gave back, who was committed to the benefit of other people. I guess you could say it was the first time I understood the importance of booking the ticket, making your commitments.

On the very first day of my Camino, I had to overcome a pretty big load of fear and misgiving. One of the main reasons I felt that fear was because of the very public commitment I had made to make this pilgrimage. Due to some difficulties

years before, which I'll explain later, I was afraid on that first
morning that I wouldn't be able to do what I had announced to
the world I was going to do. In those few, difficult moments, I
felt a bit trapped by my commitment, as if I had painted myself
into a corner from which I might not escape.

Ultimately it all worked out. I took my first step, and my
fear began to fade. But even if it hadn't, I don't think I would
ever regard my commitment as a mistake. I think that a life
lived without commitment is ultimately empty. We all have a
built-in need to believe in something—our work, our faith, our
families—and to act out that belief through commitment.

It makes sense that I needed to take that first step—and
then the ones after that—before my commitment reasserted
itself and my confidence returned. It reminds me of a maxim
by the American naturalist and writer John Burroughs: "Leap,
and the net will appear." If I had waited in that bathroom in
Saint-Jean-Pied-de-Port until I felt confident, I might never have
walked my Camino. But by starting out, even before I was sure
I could go on, I actually acquired the ability to keep walking.

In the many blogs, message boards, and other online communities centered on the Camino de Santiago, commitment is
a topic that comes up often. One blogger, Chris Reynolds, said,
"I have found that in life, when you commit to one thing—when
you are wholeheartedly committed to what you truly want—
limitless inspiration and opportunities will grow from that."
Another online writer shared, "The farther I walked, the more
my commitment grew."

Jiab Wasserman, who completed her Camino with her hus-
band in April 2019, poses the question,

Why do people commit themselves to such an arduous walk, which can take weeks to complete? In an age that provides convenience, comfort, speed and efficiency, thousands from around the globe walk hundreds of miles, enduring considerable physical demands, long periods of solitude, and deprivation from most modern comforts and conveniences. I can't answer that question for all pilgrims. But I can honestly say that it was one of the most memorable experiences of my life.

I can certainly echo Ms. Wasserman's sentiments. And it seems to me that any life-changing experience or pursuit—anything with the potential to fundamentally alter our way of seeing ourselves, others, and the world—surely requires commitment. Without commitment, does anything of enduring value ever happen? I don't think so.

When I think of the earliest days of the Camino, commitment comes into vivid focus. As I mentioned in the introduction, those ancient pilgrims didn't have the luxury of taking a flight or a train to a jumping-off point like Saint-Jean-Pied-de-Port. They had to travel hundreds of miles on foot, on horseback, or if they were lucky, in a wagon, just to get the privilege of walking the Camino. And once they reached the cathedral in Santiago de Compostela, they had to turn around and make their way home. That is real commitment!

The same could be said for the monks and others who served faithfully at the hospitals and albergues, providing aid, comfort, and often medical care to beleaguered peregrinos. Day after day, these committed servants took in people they had never seen, most of whom could probably offer nothing in exchange for the service they received. And yet for centuries, this sacred duty was passed down from generation to generation, a commitment that was first inherited, and then embodied.

HOSPITAL DE ÓRBIGO

The village of Hospital de Órbigo is located beside the Órbigo River, between the cities of León and Astorga. A stone bridge over the river at this site dates from the Middle Ages. Originally the site was occupied by a small church dedicated to the Virgin Mary, called Puente de Órbigo ("puente" means "bridge" in Spanish). In the sixteenth century, the Knights Hospitaller of St. John built a wayside hospital for the aid of pilgrims on the Camino de Santiago. The medieval bridge, built over an earlier Roman bridge, was the site of a famous and protracted jousting match in 1434, when a knight named Don Suero de Quiñones supposedly challenged all comers over a period of a month. He is said to have broken the lances of three hundred opponents in order to free himself from the bondage of a woman's unrequited love.

My Peregrino Credentials

I'll never forget how I felt in late June of 2018 when my pilgrim passport—my *credencial del peregrino*—arrived in the mail from the organization American Pilgrims on the Camino. Holding it in my hand, I had a real sense of joining a community that spanned centuries. I tried to visualize how it would look after I had passed each station of the Camino and received the official stamp on my passport, marking my progress toward the final destination at the Cathedral de Santiago.

Each passport has inscribed on it the "Pilgrim's Prayer," which dates back to the time of Pope Calixtus II, in the twelfth century:

> O God, you called your servant Abraham from Ur in Chaldea, watching over him in all his wanderings, and guided the Hebrew people as they crossed the desert. Guard these your children who, for love of your Name, make a pilgrimage to Compostela. Be their companion on the way, their guide at the crossroads, their strength in weariness, their defense in dangers, their shelter on the path, their shade in the heat, their light in darkness, their comfort in discouragement, and the firmness of their intentions, that through your guidance they may arrive safely at the end of their journey and, enriched with grace and virtue, may return to their homes filled with salutary and lasting joy.

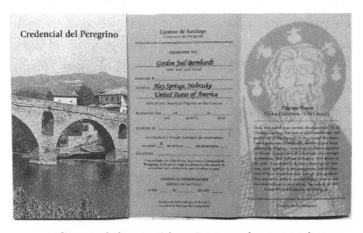

Three panels from my Pilgrim Passport when it arrived.

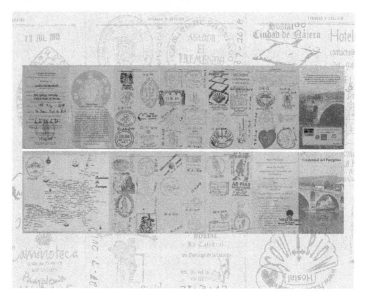

Both sides of my Pilgrim Passport after completing the Camino.

As one reads these words, one can imagine them being spoken in Spanish, in French, in German, in Italian, and in all the other languages used by the millions of pilgrims from all over the world who have made this journey. Their voices stretch back centuries. It is amazing to contemplate such an immense community, each member drawn to the others by a common commitment to journey successfully and reach the cathedral in Santiago de Compostela. It is also impressive to try imagining the millions of hopes, doubts, encouraging words, and glimpses of understanding experienced and shared by all the people who have walked this path.

Walking on that first day with Julia and then with the others, it became clear to me how important it is to be in relationship with others who share your commitments. In fact, one of the deepest lessons I learned as I walked the Camino has to do with how important relationships are to who we are and who we become. When you are on any kind of journey, whether it is physical, like the Camino, or whether it is emotional, spiritual, financial, or intellectual, there is nothing more vital than having good traveling companions. The right companions build you up, reinforce your commitments, and aid you in your travel. On the other hand, the wrong type of companions is a hindrance. They can distract, discourage, and even cause you to lose your way.

The three fellow travelers from the Fellowship who arrived in Santiago de Compostela with me. From left to right: Philipp, Astrid, me, and Julia.

I was deeply blessed by my traveling companions on the Camino. We walked together or stayed in touch for most of the way. I gradually came to think of them as my "Fellowship," much like Tolkien's *The Fellowship of the Ring*. Three of the Fellowship—Philipp and Astrid from Austria and Julia from Germany—would actually finish the Camino de Santiago at the same time I did. What a joy it was to stand with our arms across each other's shoulders in the cathedral plaza in Santiago de Compostela and celebrate the completion of our pilgrimage. Sharing this commitment as I journeyed with my Fellowship brought rewards I had never anticipated.

In the next chapter, I want to share with you some of the things I observed about relationships as I walked the Camino, both alone and with members of my Fellowship. I hope that, wherever your journey is taking you right now, you can find something to encourage you as you travel.

For Reflection

- If there are personal, professional, or financial commitments you have made or should make, what are they?

- Who are your trusted traveling companions for the journey as you seek to accomplish what is important to you and to create your legacy?

Scan to see a color image of the photos in this chapter.

CHAPTER 4

We're All Peregrinos

On July 16, 2018, I had very specific plans about how I would spend my day. I would be leaving for my Camino in two days, and I had several items on my to-do list that loomed large in my mind. Mid-morning, I had a haircut appointment, and then I needed to go home and spray my sleeping bag and backpack with permethrin, an insecticide, in case I ran into bed bugs on the Camino. I had several other activities planned, and I was pretty intent on checking off the items on my list.

But things started going awry even before I completed my first item. A little before 9:30 a.m., Nelson, my barber, texted me to ask if I could come in around 2:00 that afternoon instead of 10:30 a.m. Annoyed, I replied that I couldn't, and that I would just get my hair cut elsewhere. I could tell from his response that my reply created a problem, but I was determined to keep my day on schedule. He agreed to see me at 10:30 anyway.

After my haircut I went home to work on my gear. While I was busily engaged with that task, I got a call from the office, informing me that a good friend and client was there, hoping to bid me bon voyage. Once again, my first response was a twinge of aggravation. Why hadn't this person called to make sure I was in before showing up at my office? I told my staff I would be there as soon as possible. After finishing my equipment check, I headed for the office.

On the ten-minute drive from my house, my mind was still churning with last-minute details. I reached our building, parked, and went inside. The first thing I noticed was that there were no soft drinks in our office fridge. We typically keep it stocked for clients and other visitors while they wait. Another deviation! It was becoming harder by the minute to keep my day on track!

If I hadn't been so preoccupied with everything that wasn't going according to my plan, I would have probably noticed the sneaky smile of Zack, our colleague who sits up front and greets those who come in the door. But, unaware, I steamed ahead toward my office, ready to say my goodbyes to the client who had shown up unexpectedly.

Only when I was greeted by a loud "Surprise!" from a crowd of associates, clients, and friends gathered in the conference room did I realize that the whole thing was a setup. My team had ambushed me with a going-away party. As I stood there with a dumb grin on my face, I finally put the pieces together: the call from my barber canceling my usual haircut appointment, the summons back to the office to greet the friend and client who had dropped in. I had been suckered! I was the victim of a conspiracy, but it was a wonderful surprise.

You don't have to be headed for a six hundred-mile walk in Spain to become preoccupied. It happens to all of us, all the time: work pressures, family responsibilities, community concerns—a host of items line up every day, each one ready to shoehorn its way into our attention. And when we become preoccupied, we fail to notice so much that is going on around us. Most critically perhaps, we fail to notice the people in our lives.

Invitation to my going-away party.

The fact is that we are all on a journey together; we are all fellow pilgrims—peregrinos and peregrinas. And I'm not just talking about friends, family members, and other people we highly regard (at least, most of the time). I'm also talking about those people in our lives who always have something to complain about: that relative who makes a scene at family gatherings; that boss who refuses to cut anyone any slack; that acquaintance who always shows up at the most inconvenient moment needing help. We are all in relationship as we move through life, and that can be pleasant or challenging, sustaining or draining, a source of joy or a source of anxiety. Sometimes it can be all of these at once.

I love what British philosopher and author C. S. Lewis says about our relationships with the people in our lives:[6]

> There are no *ordinary* people. You have never talked to a mere mortal. Nations, cultures, arts, civilization—these are mortal, and their life is to ours as the life of a gnat. But it is immortals whom we joke with, work with, marry, snub, and exploit—immortal horrors or everlasting splendors...your neighbor is the holiest object presented to your senses.

Lewis's words really ring true for me, and my experiences on the Camino de Santiago reinforced the sentiment. When my team at Bernhardt Wealth Management scuttled my plans for the day by honoring me with a going-away party, they were teaching me—again—about the immeasurable value of relationships—all relationships. On my Facebook entry for that day, beside a picture of the sneaky invitation they sent out to various friends and clients, I wrote this about my team: "I can't believe I get to work side-by-side with people smarter and better than me and that we get the pleasure of serving our great clients. Thanks for the nice surprise and gift. Thank you, Tim, Solon, Bonnie, Chay, Cameron, Susan, Olivia, Zachary, and Austin. And thanks for showing up to celebrate, Sally, Peter, and Regina. It was a great surprise!"

Our relationships are the most precious things we have. Beyond money, beyond influence, beyond fame or professional success, we are truly defined by the quality of our relationships. And our web of relationships extends outward in ways that we don't always realize.

---

6   C. S. Lewis, *The Weight of Glory* (New York: The MacMillan Company, 1949).

Me in my travel gear with my teammates, prior to departure.

On the Camino de Santiago, this truth manifests itself in very practical ways, almost every day. I remember that on July 21, 2018, I was walking from Roncesvalles to Zubiri. The albergue I had stayed at the night before happened to be staffed by volunteers from the Netherlands, and I remember particularly how kind and helpful they were to me and my fellow peregrinos. By the time we finished breakfast, there was a light drizzle, so we put on our ponchos before we started walking.

About halfway through the distance I planned to cover that day, I stopped at a café to wait for some of my Fellowship to catch up. The routine I established on the Camino was to start walking around 6:30 a.m., before sunrise, and cover a few miles before stopping to have breakfast. Some peregrinos, including some in my Fellowship, started earlier than me, and some later. In fact, it's pretty common on the Camino to not be constantly with your companions; everyone understands that people walk at different paces, and as often as not, we meet back up at some point on the day's hike. It's just another way of "walking your own Camino."

This circumstance often caused me to reflect on the fluidity of relationships: people come in and out of our lives at various times, and we go in and out of theirs, but our paths may cross on multiple occasions. It's interesting to think about why this is the case, and whether the people who happen to be in our circle at any given moment are in some way the people we need, just as we may be the person they need.

Later that day, after I rejoined Julia, Astrid, and Tanja, the four of us met Stéphane, from France. He told us that earlier that day, while he was taking a rest break, he lost his wallet. What happened next is a perfect example of the importance of the invisible web of relationships, especially on the Camino de Santiago. Here's what I wrote about it on my Facebook page for that day:

> A few miles later he realized he lost it and walked back asking people he met if they had seen it. Word spread like wildfire and eventually Stéphane was reunited with his wallet, which had been picked up by another pilgrim. I don't know if there is a pilgrim's code, but that pilgrim's actions exemplified the best of humanity and left the rest of us feeling good. Over dinner that evening, it was amazing how many stopped and asked about the wallet.

I think we all love stories like this: circumstances that display the best of human nature. And these stories also remind us that every time we take a moment to help someone else, even if it's someone we don't know, we strengthen the positive ties that bind us all together as fellow travelers, pilgrims on the journey of life.

Kindness, consideration, empathy for a fellow human being, basic honesty—actions motivated by these impulses are never wasted.

On the other hand, that very same day, I witnessed a less enjoyable aspect of that invisible web of relationships as I walked through various pastures along the route. I wrote: "I was a little disappointed when I would see a gate in the fence for the pilgrims' convenience that was not securely closed as it meant livestock could potentially escape. All I could do was hope the pilgrim behind me would close it securely like I had."

If you have ever spent much time in the farming and ranching country of rural America, you know the unwritten rule: "If you open a gate, close it behind you." This rule holds whether you're in the swampy lowland ranches of Louisiana, the arid plains of West Texas, or the high country of Montana.

As a boy growing up in northwestern Nebraska, I have many memories of riding across pastureland in my dad's pickup. When we came to a gate, it was my job as the passenger to hop out, open the gate, let my dad drive through, then close and latch the gate behind the pickup before hopping back in the cab. All our neighbors knew and obeyed this rule, too. If you've ever leased land for hunting or even taken a casual drive with a farmer or rancher along a field road, you've learned the importance of making sure that the livestock don't wander through an open gate to someplace their owner doesn't want them to be.

As I walked from Roncesvalles to Zubiri that day, I came upon many gates in pasture fences or walls. They were there as a courtesy to the peregrinos traveling the Camino, but many of them were carelessly left open. I think this may have been one of the more annoying things I encountered on what was otherwise a generally uplifting and satisfying Camino journey.

My father was a big believer in taking good care of other people's property. In fact, as I look back, he may have been a little bit obsessive about it. If he borrowed a hand tool, he would return it cleaned, sharpened, oiled, or otherwise in its best possible condition. If a shovel had a cracked handle, Dad would put a new handle on it. If he borrowed a tractor, it had a full tank of gas when it went back to its owner. And you already know that he never left an unlatched gate behind him.

Me with my father in Texas for the wedding of my niece, March 17, 2018.

Relationships with neighbors mattered to my dad. He intuitively understood that we are all fellow peregrinos, and we have to do what we can to take care of each other.

I think this idea makes sense to most people, and indeed, most of the world's great religions teach some form of this principle. The Golden Rule is familiar to many of us who remember what Jesus said in the New Testament: "Do to others as you would want them to do to you." But many may not be aware that a Buddhist writing from the sixth century BC says, "Hurt not others with that which pains yourself." Similarly, Mohammed taught, "You do not have faith until you love for others what you love for yourself." A Hindu teaching from around 3,200 BC says, "One should always treat others as they themselves wish to be treated." And, as written in the Jewish scriptures of the Old Testament, "You should love your neighbor as yourself." Throughout the centuries, people of good will the world over have understood that we are all walking together on the common road of humanity. The more we can recognize each other as fellow travelers, the better the journey will be for all of us.

It isn't always easy to do that, of course. Maybe that's why almost every religion carries some reminder of our mutual responsibility to each other. If it always came naturally, we wouldn't need so many memos from our spiritual forebears!

Lots of obstacles can prevent us from staying aware of our many interconnected relationships. As I mentioned at the beginning of this chapter, sometimes we get distracted managing the details of our lives. We get task-focused and situation-focused and lose our ability to truly recognize the people around us. Other times the particular relationship may pose its own obstacles. Let's face it: there are people in our lives who are simply more difficult to be in relationship with than others! All of us go through times in our journey when stress or grief or another difficult emotional passage knocks us off the trail for a while.

The trail to Santiago de Compostela sometimes led through pasturelands. If a careless pilgrim leaves a gate open, the livestock can wander off!

Whatever the circumstances, the need to have good traveling companions—and to be good companions for each other—never goes away. Whether we walk in rain, as we did part of that day from Roncesvalles to Zubiri, or in sunshine; in good times and bad; whether downhill or up a steep grade, the journey always goes easier and safer when we're with other peregrinos.

That doesn't mean, of course, that there won't always be a need for flexibility in giving and receiving. I often reflected on this as I thought about my Fellowship and our mutual journey. There were times when we walked together, and there were times when we were separated. I deeply valued both conditions. There was an agreement among us that each of us might need to walk at a different pace for a given time. We were each walking our own Camino.

Joyce Rupp makes a similar point in her book *Walk in a Relaxed Manner*.[7] Though she and her friend of twenty years, Father Tom Pfeffer, had decided to stay together for their entire time on the Camino de Santiago, she noticed many other pilgrims who, for various reasons, made a different decision. "The Camino can bring out the best and the worst in a pilgrim," she writes.

> All sorts of things come rising to the surface in the continuous rhythm of walking. This obviously influences how two people get along. As in daily life, no one can plan for this ahead of time. There has to be openness to what might arise for both self and the other person. If the pilgrims are wise they will agree not to take it personally if the other person decides to walk on alone.

I was glad that in my Fellowship, this need for give and take—for times of solitude alternating with hours of companionship—never seemed an obstacle. Rather, it was just one more blessing that made the Camino de Santiago such a transforming experience for me.

---

7   Rupp, *Walk in a Relaxed Manner*.

As I mentioned in the opening pages of this book, I am fine when I have no company other than myself. I did all of my training walks alone, except for occasional encounters with people I met on the trail. The steady rhythm of walking helps me focus on each moment while also allowing me time to reflect on the day, my work, various relationships, and other worthwhile matters. On the Camino, I started many days of walking by myself in the darkness of predawn. I relished those times of quiet reflection. In fact, I often received insights and thoughts as I walked in solitude at different times of the day.

On the other hand, when I was walking with members of my Fellowship or other pilgrims I met along the Camino, I almost always received a gift from the insights, observations, and attitudes they provided, different from the gifts I received when walking alone. I already mentioned how Julia from Munich, on that first day as I took my initial and somewhat hesitant steps, provided the perfect encouragement that helped me move forward with confidence. And I would like to think that I was a help on her first day, as well. I learned so much from fellow travelers like Ole from Denmark, a seventy-year-old veteran of multiple Caminos, and from the twelve-year-old Italian girl walking the Camino with her family.

I was even encouraged by pilgrims I never actually saw. One of the practices I enjoyed the most on the Camino was the way pilgrims leave notes of encouragement for each other on rocks, posts, signs, and other prominent places along the trail.

Don't STOP Walking.

Do It with Love.

Free Hugs.

Never Give Up on the Good Things.

Like the many statues and other depictions of pilgrims, both ancient and modern, that lined the Camino, these little messages reminded me that I was in a network of relationships that spanned geography and even time. Each time I remembered this, it was another encouragement to keep going. It was also a reminder of the importance of providing that same encouragement to others.

When I think of the relationships in my life that are most important, I'm typically also aware of how grateful I am for these people and what they mean to me. When I posted on Facebook about my surprise going-away party, I mentioned how thankful I was for my team. In fact, it would be hard for me to adequately express my gratitude for them and the way they take care of our clients—and each other!

Recognizing what we should be grateful for and cultivating a spirit of gratitude may be the single biggest factor that separates people who are happy and fulfilled from those who aren't. On the Camino de Santiago, I had many opportunities to reflect on gratitude and thankfulness, and next, I'd like to tell you about a few of them.

For Reflection

- Who are some of the people in your life who have made the greatest difference?

- What is the difference between having dependable traveling companions and following the crowd?

Scan to see a color image of the photos in this chapter.

CHAPTER 5

Too Grateful to Worry

The final part of the journey to the Cathedral de Santiago de Compostela lies along a path that weaves among groves of eucalyptus trees. I was walking with three of the original members of my Fellowship: Astrid, Philipp, and Julia. Earlier we had committed to walking together into the city and to the plaza of the Cathedral, which would represent the culmination of our pilgrimage.

The shade of the eucalyptus trees was pleasant—it can be quite warm in August, even in northern Spain—and the clean, astringent fragrance of eucalyptus filled our noses as we approached the greatly anticipated end of our journey together. We had started walking at five o'clock that morning from Salceda, a town about twenty-seven kilometers—just over seventeen miles—from our final destination. We had just descended the valley of the Río Sionlla, the final stream crossed by pilgrims on the Camino Francés before entering Santiago de Compostela. In older times, pilgrims would perform ceremonial washings in the small waterway, giving the place its current name, Lavacolla. If you've studied Spanish, you can probably figure out the name refers to washing your hind parts. We opted to skip this particular tradition on our way to the Cathedral.

After crossing the stream, we began our final climb, which took us up the slope of Monte do Gozo—"Hill of Joy" in the Galician dialect of this region of Spain. The hill is so named because when pilgrims reach its peak, they have their first view down into Santiago de Compostela, and the spires of the Cathedral de Santiago de Compostela are finally revealed. The peregrino's joy and gratitude at the sight of the long-sought destination is captured in the statues of the Memorial to the Pilgrim.

The Monument to the Pilgrim at Monte do Gozo offers the first view of the spires of the cathedral in Santiago de Compostela.

The Monument to the Pilgrim at Monte do Gozo shows the euphoria of two pilgrims when they see the spires of the cathedral in Santiago de Compostela.

Approaching from behind the statues, it is easy to imagine the gratitude of the two pilgrims, depicted as they first catch sight of the spires of the cathedral and raise their hands in a gesture of thankfulness. I certainly felt that way, walking with my companions on that hot August day.

In fact, I would say that on most of my days on the Camino, I was conscious of a great sense of gratitude. At the same time that doesn't mean every day was easy or that I didn't encounter obstacles, both inner and outer. One of the things I learned is that gratitude doesn't necessarily depend on things being easy. I thought about this a lot while I was walking across the Meseta.

"The Sublime Meseta"

I remember the first time I heard other peregrinos talking about the Meseta, the name given to the huge plateau that constitutes much of central Spain. Somewhat like the plains of the western United States, the Meseta is a region known for little shade, flat terrain, lots of sky, and long distances between towns. When I reached Burgos, about a third of the way through the route, I began overhearing worried conversations about the Meseta. Even Philipp, one of the peregrinos in my Fellowship, called the Meseta a "desert" and wondered how we would manage to cross it, since the Camino Francés lies across its northern reaches.

I replied, somewhat flippantly, that I was going to "grab the Meseta by the throat and subdue it," but I also couldn't help wondering how, in all the planning and reading I had done, I had managed to overlook a region that was apparently so problematic. Was the Meseta really going to be that difficult?

I left Burgos on August 1, 2018, to set out across the Meseta, and I would finish crossing it about the time I reached Astorga, about 232 kilometers (144 miles) on the walking route. As I started walking that day, I have to admit that while I still felt confident, I was wondering why so many fellow travelers held such negative impressions of the region we were walking through.

Here is what I wrote on my Facebook page after the first day of walking across the Meseta:

> I mentioned yesterday that all day I heard various pilgrims talk about the terrible Meseta. Some referred to it as a desert. I heard another pilgrim mention she heard travelers should not walk alone, as they may be ambushed. And I kept telling people I was going to grab the Meseta by the throat and subdue it. However, I must confess that those expressed fears planted a seed

of doubt in my mind. I kept asking myself how I overlooked the dreaded Meseta.

And on the first third of today's walk, two things came
to mind. First, I realized it takes a lot of work to remove
negativity from your mind once someone plants that
seed. I kept trying to push those negative thoughts out of
my mind but they continued to surface. But on the walk
I gave thanks that I am not a person prone to negativity
and fearfulness.

The second thing I realized was how important it was to
only allow people in your inner circle who support and
encourage you. This is true for me and made me give
thanks for the business leaders, leadership team, and
friends in my life. It is also extremely important for our
youth. We want our youth to be surrounded by people
who encourage them to shoot for the stars. As the adage
goes, "You can't soar with the eagles if you're hanging
out with the turkeys."

To summarize, I conquered the first day of the Meseta,
and I plan on doing the same for the next nine days as
I walk through the Meseta.

It interested me to realize that my initial response to the
Meseta was gratitude. I suppose that was largely because despite
all the dire warnings, I found the Meseta to have its own special
type of beauty and peace. In fact, I noticed that in Brierley's
guidebook, he first refers to it as "the sublime Meseta." True,

it could get hot out there; many days the temperature reached well into the nineties. But as long as I had plenty of water and paced myself, I didn't find the Meseta to be nearly as formidable as others had made it sound. I suppose that in some way, meeting this challenge successfully also contributed to my gratitude.

The Meseta didn't look at all like a desert to me. For a guy who grew up in the wheat farming and cattle country of northwest Nebraska, much about the Meseta reminded me of home. There were broad stretches of wheat fields, and one day I walked past a farmer driving a combine. That took me back to lots of memories of watching my dad and others in our community harvesting the wheat crop.

A combine harvesting wheat on my first day in the Meseta.

In my line of work there is certainly plenty of room for negativity and worst-case-scenario thinking, if a person wants to engage in it. The financial markets are inherently unpredictable, and on some occasions adverse price movements can suck value out of a client's portfolio at an alarming rate. Not only that, but the financial media often seem bent on magnifying every trend with headlines that predict darkest disaster or unimaginable prosperity—sometimes on the same day.

Just as with my experience on the first day of walking the Meseta, reality often proves much more manageable than predictions. In fact, we routinely counsel our clients against making financial decisions based on the frequently overblown claims of media headlines, whether they are negative or positive. I found in this another reason to be grateful. As I mentioned earlier, I'm grateful for my associates at work, as well as colleagues in my Vistage CEO group, and the other people who are so important in my life.

Overwhelmingly, these are people with positive, forward-thinking attitudes who resist negativity and spend most of their time encouraging me, each other, our clients, and everyone around them. As I walked along, past sunflower fields and wheat fields, past small villages almost hidden from the road and through larger towns, I was continually reminded of how much I have to be grateful for, especially in my relationships. The more I thought about this, the less I worried about the Meseta—or anything else!

Despite all this, it occurred to me just how easy it is to allow negativity and worry to take root in our minds. I've had so many conversations with clients or colleagues where someone overheard a rumor at a cocktail party or happy hour indicating problems in some sector of the investment world. On the one hand, I'm happy when clients bring such concerns to me or my associates, because then we have the opportunity to consider everything in the light of reliable research and the bigger picture.

Such conversations almost always result in a better informed, less worried client. Having better, more complete information often relieves our worries.

However, I have concerns, as I mentioned in my Facebook post, for the effects of negative messages and influences on our young people. I think a lot about this because of my nephews and nieces: the type of world they will inherit as adults, the kind of people they will become, the opportunities—or lack thereof—that they will experience. It is so important for those of us with a bit more experience in the world to think about how we can encourage and mentor younger folks. They are not only our future; in many ways, they are our present, too. And they deserve the very best, most affirming foundation we can build for them.

One of the many resolutions I made as I walked the Camino de Santiago was to become a better encourager. After all, when gratitude is shared, it makes more for everybody.

I learned a great deal about the importance of shared gratitude from Tonnie, a fellow peregrino from the Netherlands. Like the pilgrims of ancient times, Tonnie began his Camino when he walked out his front door at home in April 2018. By the time I arrived in July, he was making his way along the Camino Francés, as I was. I will always be grateful that we shared the path, as I learned so much from him. Here is what I wrote on my Facebook page for August 5, 2018, my fifth day of walking the Meseta:

> Day 17 was a great day. I feel so blessed and grateful for so many things. Let me explain my gratitude a little more. A pilgrim told me recently that he was told by a former Camino pilgrim that there are three parts to the

Camino. Part one is the first week, when the Camino breaks you physically. Part two is the next week, when it breaks your spirit. And part three is the remainder of time, when it rebuilds you. And I can see and understand that in many ways. However, I feel a little guilty because I have loved every day and have been grateful for every day. I have had blisters but not to the extent of some others I have met. And I told friends before leaving America that I was sure there were days my body would be screaming at me for deciding to walk the Camino. There have been tough days, but even in the heat and difficulty I still have a grateful heart and don't feel my body or spirit was broken once. As crazy as it sounds, I think I will miss walking and experiencing the Camino when I reach my turnaround point to get to Madrid to catch my flight back toward the end of the month.

But back to today. I walked 16.03 miles from Moratinos to Calzadilla de los Hermanillos. I ran into Tonnie while I was having breakfast and had the privilege of walking with him for approximately the last ten miles. I can tell you that Tonnie is a gift to everyone on the Camino, and I am very grateful to have the opportunity to share things with him and to hear more of his story.

As I mentioned earlier, Tonnie began his Camino on April 30 as he left his front door in the Netherlands. I learned today that he was the youngest of four kids—one girl and three boys. I learned a lot about his character as he told me stories of various experiences in his adult life...

We also continued our conversation about relationships, personally and professionally. Overall, Tonnie was the Camino's gift to me today. I can only hope I am a gift to others in the same way…

My experiences and conversations with Tonnie reminded me that so often, the greatest gifts in our lives—the things we should be most grateful for—are the people we meet and the stories they tell us. And as I reflect on my journey, I think it is particularly significant that I recognized my gratitude perhaps most strongly while I was crossing the Meseta. I'm not sure about everyone's experience, but as I think about my own life, it occurs to me that maybe we need challenges in our lives because they make us more conscious of all we have to be grateful for. I know that my life would certainly be poorer had I never crossed the Meseta, and especially had I never met Tonnie.

Steps Taken in Gratitude

I think we all have a Meseta lying before us from time to time. Yours may not be a five- or six-day walk across a hot, arid plain. Instead, it may be a particular challenge you are facing at work. It may be a relationship that is in difficulty, financial uncertainty, or any number of other circumstances that give you pause and make you wonder if you're really up to the task. I have certainly faced all of these in my life, and sometimes I didn't do as well as when I walked the Meseta with Tonnie and other pilgrims. But I think I have learned that no matter what the issue is before me, I can deal with it more effectively if I can maintain a sense of gratitude.

When walking the Meseta, as on the rest of the journey, I really did have a sense of receiving what I needed for each day, whether that meant climbing a steep hill in ninety-degree heat or the encouragement of Tonnie's companionship and conversation. Again and again the Camino gave me what I needed—in some cases, even if I would have preferred something else!

Receiving each day, each circumstance as a gift helped me cultivate a better and more vigorous response of gratitude in every situation. Without a doubt, steps taken in gratitude are the easiest steps of all.

Of course when you are truly open to receiving everything as a gift, you may get some gifts that surprise you. The gift for that day may come in a shape, in a size, or at a time that doesn't seem particularly "gifty" at the moment. I suppose it's all about balancing expectations with perceptions.

Other times, the gift for the day may come as a chance for the unexpected, a diversion from the steady pace of the trail—even a detour to take the scenic route. On the Camino de Santiago, there are many opportunities for a peregrino to make side trips here and there in order to experience or to see something a bit off the beaten path. Some of these opportunities are easier to anticipate than others. The guidebook I followed had frequent suggestions for interesting sites that could be visited if one was willing to make a slight diversion from the planned route.

When you're on foot, of course, "a slight diversion" takes on an extra layer of meaning. After all, it's not simply a matter of a quick turn of the wheel and a few minutes of driving, then back to the highway. Walking long distances, especially with a specific goal in mind, entails planning and, above all, careful attention to expenditure of resources—water, nourishment, footing, and one's available stamina. There's really no such thing as "a quick side trip" when you're on a long-distance hike like the Camino de Santiago.

But does that mean you should always stick to the trail? What might you be missing if you just walk doggedly forward each day, not allowing yourself to look left or right to see what unexpected things might be available? I can honestly say that I experienced both sides of this decision as I walked my Camino; there were times when I took a side road and was grateful for it, and there were other times when I didn't and felt twinges of regret for what I might have missed.

We all face similar decisions, every day of our lives, and we never really know if it's worth it until after we've made our choice. In the next few pages I'll tell you a few stories of both outcomes from my walk in Spain.

For Reflection

- What is the difference between worry and planning responsibly for the future?

- What are the main differences you observe between people who are grateful and those who are not?

Scan to see a color image of the photos in this chapter.

CHAPTER 6

The Castle at
the Top of the Hill

At the end of my first day walking the Meseta, I arrived in the village of Hontanas, a tiny community that seems almost hidden among the vastness of the surrounding plains. I was glad to arrive there, certainly, but because Hontanas was built in a small valley, there is no visible sign of the place until you are almost upon it. I'm not the first to notice this fact.

In the 1670s an Italian pilgrim, Domenico Laffi, wrote, "With God's help we crossed this deserted wasteland and reached the village of Hontanas. It lies hidden in the valley of a little river, so that you scarcely see it until you have reached it."

In the photograph I took as I reached Hontanas, you can get a sense of the sweep of the Meseta with this small village nestled down in the midst of it. I would guess that Hontanas has probably changed very little in the 350 years since Laffi recorded his observations.

The village of Hontanas.

My plan for the next day was to walk to Boadilla del Camino, another small town about thirty kilometers (18.65 miles) away. It was hot on the Meseta, and though my first day had restored my confidence, I still knew it was important to mind my capabilities. So I set out from Hontanas on the morning of August 2 with Boadilla del Camino firmly fixed as my goal for the day's walk.

After about ten kilometers (a little over six miles), I came to the village of Castrojeriz. On a hill high above the town crouch the ruins of the Castillo de San Esteban, a medieval fortress that is said to have been built on the site of a much older Roman fortification called Castrum Sigerici. On its steep hilltop, commanding a wide view of the surrounding plains, it's easy to see why someone would want to fortify this location. In the medieval period it was an important stop along the pilgrimage route, perhaps because of the protection afforded by the castle and its garrison. The town is said to have supported eight pilgrim hospitals at one time. Now, however, many of them have fallen into ruin, much like the castle.

The Castillo de San Esteban on the hill above Iglesia de Santa María del Manzano.

I still had the majority of my day's walking ahead of me, but as I approached Castrojeriz and contemplated the castle at the top of the hill, I imagined what things would look like from up there. Before long I was seriously contemplating a detour from my planned route to see for myself. Then I began thinking about how far I still had to go that day, how hot it was getting, and all the other steep hills I had to climb, including the 900-meter Alto de Mostelares, just on the other side of Castrojeriz. Ultimately I talked myself out of making the climb up to the castle. But the idea never quite left my mind.

Once I got back home after my Camino, as I was going through my many photographs and posting them on Facebook, I once again came across the pictures I took as I was passing through Castrojeriz and the Castillo de San Esteban. I promised myself that one of these years I'm going to go back there. I'm going to take that side road to the top of the hill and see the view from the castle.

There was another occasion almost two weeks later, as I neared Santiago de Compostela, when I faced a similar choice on my route to the town of Sarria. Here's what I wrote in my Facebook diary on August 15, 2018:

I left at 6:30 a.m. today and it was pitch black. It was the first day I had to use my headlamp to find and see the markers. I had two choices today in terms of how to get to Sarria. One was a scenic view and the other was also a scenic view that was 6.5 kilometers longer but included walking by an old monastery. I kept telling myself to take the shorter route since I am this close to Santiago. Over and over, I kept saying take the shorter route. Guess which one I took? Yes, the longer route.

The photo I am posting is one from the trail. There were times I walked on the side of roads and times I walked on trails like this. Of course, I have no way of knowing whether that route was more scenic. But my gift from the Camino was to meet Armando and Elvira from Las Vegas. They both immigrated to the US from the Philippines over thirty years ago. They are engineers and retired four years ago and moved from the San Francisco area to Las Vegas a year ago.

They have been planning their Camino for a year and were diligently walking [before coming to Spain] to prepare for their walk on the Camino. Unfortunately, Elvira injured her heel a few weeks before they arrived.

They had planned to walk the entire Camino like I am doing but the injury means they are walking slower and took a bus for a lot of it. They think they can walk the remainder if they do it in small doses...

A view of the trail to Samos and the old monastery.

I chose what I thought would be the more scenic route, even though it was an additional six and a half kilometers (about four miles). I'm so glad I did! Not only did I get to see the monastery, which was lovely, I also enjoyed walking through the village of Samos, where the monastery is located. In Samos there were bridges with railings decorated in wrought iron scallop shells, one of the symbols of the Camino de Santiago.

But even more important than the scenery was the chance I had to meet and walk three miles with Armando and Elvira, two of the nicest and most positive people I have ever met.

The Samos monastery in the village of Samos.

The Samos Monastery as seen through a scallop shell on a nearby bridge.

The scallop shell bridge over the Río Sarria near the Samos monastery.

When you decide to take the scenic route, there's no telling what you'll find. Had I opted to climb the hill to Castillo de San Esteban at Castrojeriz, Brierley's guidebook assured me of "fine views and sunsets." When I was passing through, it was the wrong time of day for a sunset view, but maybe the panorama from atop the ruined castle wall would have been worth it anyway. One day I'll find out for myself.

What is it that causes us to choose the more direct path over the scenic route? Obviously, when we're in a hurry, we opt for the fastest way. There are certainly situations where time is of the essence and the scenic route is a poor choice. But I sometimes wonder, in our fast-paced, modern lives, how often we allow ourselves to be in a hurry even when we have a choice to do otherwise. What might we miss in those times, as we rush from one appointment to the next? Maybe it's better to ask: What might we gain if we allowed ourselves to take the scenic route?

One answer might be better mental and emotional health. According to a study published in the December 2018 issue of the journal *Environment International*, commuters whose route to work regularly included natural elements like trees, open fields, or streams scored higher on a mental health evaluation than those whose routes were in more urban, non-natural settings. Researchers studied 3,599 active commuters from cities in Spain, the Netherlands, Lithuania, and the United Kingdom, and the results were consistent across all groups. In fact, those who walked or biked through such settings—as opposed to driving a car through them—scored even higher on the mental health screening.

One of the authors of the study is quoted as saying, "From previous experimental studies we knew that physical activity in natural environments can reduce stress and improve mood and mental restoration when compared to the equivalent activity in urban environments...our data show that commuting through these natural spaces alone may also have a positive effect on mental health."[8]

To me that's not surprising. One of the greatest benefits of my long-distance walking has been the chance to get away from the streets, the noise, and the hurried pace of the city. When you are walking—and probably when you are cycling (but not in a race)—you notice more of your surroundings. You become more aware of changes in elevation, bends in the road, the sounds around you. You can actually see the faces of the people with whom you share the trail. It becomes much easier to truly enter

---

8   Wilma L. Zijlema, et al., "Active Commuting through Natural Environments is Associated with Better Mental Health: Results from the PHENOTYPE Project," *Environmental International* 121, no. 1 (2018): 721–727, https://www.sciencedirect.com/science/article/pii/S0160412018313667.

each moment and absorb all the experiences it offers. I think that when we do this, we become more fully human. It makes perfect sense to me that it also makes us more mentally healthy.

I think that many of those who have walked the Camino de Santiago have discovered something similar. I can't help believing that this principle—slowing down and allowing yourself scenic detours—lies behind the impact that the Camino has on the lives of those who experience it.

Several months after I returned from my pilgrimage—on Super Bowl Sunday, 2019—I found something that I had apparently been carrying with me on the Camino that I didn't know I had. In itself that's not surprising, since in many of the villages where I stopped, the hosts at the albergues or even people at the churches would hand out various keepsakes or other mementos to peregrinos. But when I found this particular item, an anonymous blessing of encouragement, it really struck a chord with me, because in so many ways, it captures the whole idea of the unexpected blessings and benefits that come to you on the Camino de Santiago. It's called "The Beatitudes of the Pilgrim":

Blessed are you, pilgrim, if you discover that the
*   Camino opens your eyes to what is not seen.*
Blessed are you, pilgrim, if what concerns you most is
*   not to arrive, but to arrive with others.*
Blessed are you, pilgrim, when you contemplate the
*   Camino and you discover it is full of names and*
*   dawns.*
Blessed are you, pilgrim, because you have discovered
*   that the authentic Camino begins when it is*
*   completed.*

*Blessed are you, pilgrim, if you discover that one
   step back to help another is more valuable than a
   hundred forward without seeing who or what is
   by your side.*
*Blessed are you, pilgrim, when you don't have words
   to give thanks for everything that surprises you at
   every twist and turn along the way.*
*Blessed are you, pilgrim, if you search for the truth
   and make of the Camino a life of your life.*
*Blessed are you, pilgrim, if on the way you meet
   yourself and gift yourself with time, without
   rushing, so as not to disregard the image in your
   heart.*
*Blessed are you, pilgrim, if you discover that the
   Camino holds a lot of silence; and the silence of
   prayer, and the prayer of meeting God, who is
   waiting for you.*

Parts of this beautiful benediction are almost like a philoso-phy of taking the scenic route: "...the Camino opens your eyes to what is not seen...to give thanks for everything that surprises you at every twist and turn...gift yourself with time...so as not to disregard the image in your heart..." These phrases ring true in a way that is hard to explain to anyone who has not walked the Camino or had a similar life-changing experience.

They also remind me powerfully of the importance of really seeing; not just going through your day with your eyes always fixed on the next task, but actually seeing the things and people around you. I think part of that mindset involves a willingness to sometimes take the scenic route. I believe that sometimes, in order to find what we're really looking for, we have to be diverted from the path we're on. If you really buy into the concept that "the Camino gives you what you need," then the logical next step is to accept everything you receive, every experience you have—however unexpected—as something necessary for the true completion of your pilgrimage.

"The End of the World"

One more story about scenic detours from my time on the Camino comes to mind, and it seems appropriate here. Actually this occurred after I had made it to Santiago de Compostela and was on my walk to Cape Finisterre, the site on the Atlantic coast that the Romans called "the end of the world."

I had just left Muxía, a town just north of Cape Finisterre, when a local man stopped me. He could tell I was a peregrino, and he obviously really wanted to tell me something, though he spoke very little English. Here is what I wrote in my Facebook entry for August 23, 2018:

> When I left Muxía yesterday a local Spanish man stopped me. It was clear he was trying to be helpful, but I spoke no Spanish and he spoke no English. However, I am pretty sure he was telling me there were two routes to Finisterre—a more direct one or the scenic one that followed the coast. He was advising me to go right and take the scenic path.

I knew there was a coastal path. As much as I wanted to take the coastal path, I wasn't interested in multiplying the distance to Finisterre by a factor of 1.5 to 2 times. I shook his hand and thanked him for his advice.

Why am I closing a chapter on taking the scenic route with another example of a time when I didn't? I think it is because in this instance, I realized on some level that my entire journey in Spain—which was coming to a close—had been one long scenic route. By the time I reached the cape "at the end of the world," I would have spent more than a month during which every day had afforded me multiple opportunities for quiet reflection; contemplation of the slowly passing scenery; honest, unhurried conversations with my fellow pilgrims; and the opportunity to experience life in a way that was more elemental, basic, and freeing than anything I had ever known.

I think that by this point in my Camino, I was ready to evaluate the real benefit of taking the side road instead of the more direct route. There was something in me that really wanted to take the scenic path along the coast, but, as I had written earlier in my entry for that day:

After walking for thirty-five days and staying in places with no amenities and normally hot rooms, I am ready for a more relaxing experience as I decompress and reflect. I take the train to Madrid on August 29 and fly back on August 30. I will stop by the office on the 30th but will not even look at my desk or email until I return after Labor Day.

In other words, I was already on the scenic route, and in many ways, I'm still on it today! True to my word, even after I was back in the United States, I did not allow myself to look at the thousands of emails in my inbox or listen to the voice messages on my phone. I needed time, now that I was finished walking the physical Camino, to assess, reflect, and absorb the inner, emotional, and spiritual Camino. I needed to fully appreciate all I had seen on my slightly more than month-long scenic detour.

I will probably be assessing and learning from my Camino for the rest of my life. And it seems to me that this is just as it should be. Walking the Camino de Santiago was—and continues to be—a deeply fulfilling experience. But as I related at the beginning of the book, I was not always so sure I would be able to complete the journey.

On the first day as I was setting out, I had tremendous doubts about my ability, and even wondered if I had made a huge mistake by attempting this. The reason for all these difficult feelings is rooted in a story of failure that had occurred years before. And yet, in a strange way, I now believe that failure was essential to my ultimate success on the Camino. So I'd like to tell you about it and suggest why I now believe you should never allow failure to define you.

....

For Reflection

- What was the last unplanned "side trip" you made? What were your main takeaways?

- What is your attitude toward changes in your plans? Do you usually find them annoying, or are they interesting?

....

Scan to see a color image of the photos in this chapter.

CHAPTER 7

If You Really Want to Succeed, You've Got to Fail

In 2015, as I was already contemplating walking the Camino de Santiago, I decided to walk the entire length of the C&O Canal, which runs 184.5 miles from Washington, DC to Cumberland, Maryland. Its actual name is the Chesapeake and Ohio Canal, originally constructed between 1828 and 1850, mainly to transport coal from the Allegheny Mountains along the Potomac River valley to the nation's capital. The original plan was to connect it to the Ohio River at Pittsburgh, which gave the "Grand Old Ditch" the second part of its name. However, that part of the canal was never built.

There is a great hiking and biking trail that runs the length of the canal, a perfect route. I told lots of people what I intended to do, and I took a train to Cumberland, full of confidence, looking forward to completing the hike. But after only four days and about ninety miles, I had to stop; my feet were in such tremendous pain that I couldn't go on.

The towpath that runs along the C&O Canal.

As I would later learn, I had a foot condition called hammertoes: an abnormal bend in the middle joint that forces the end of the toe down at an angle. The unnatural position of the toe makes it susceptible to pain when walking—as I learned all too well after four days of walking the C&O Canal.

For obvious reasons, this experience was etched in my mind as the time drew nearer for my Camino. I began experimenting with different kinds of shoes, socks, orthotic supports, and anything else I could find that would enable me to walk long distances without pain. I made multiple trips to REI to try on different hiking shoes, and I turned several pairs back in immediately because they didn't feel right. I probably went through six or seven pairs of shoes before I found the ones—Brooks Caldera 2 Trail-Running Shoe—that were comfortable and sturdy enough to keep my feet in good shape for the long haul. The REI employee informed me that this particular Brooks shoe had a specially designed bubble built into the heel to absorb shock while walking. That was fine, but the main thing was that these shoes, in combination with the orthotic support and the particular socks I finally settled on, allowed me to walk without pain.

Still, even after all that, on the first morning of my Camino as I prepared to set out from Saint-Jean-Pied-de-Port to cross the Pyrenees into Spain, I was still troubled by my failure in 2015. I remembered the unbearable pain in my feet and the embarrassment of failing to do what I had announced to so many friends. That troubling memory is what caused me to hug the toilet, wishing I could throw up and get rid of the discomfort in my stomach. I'll always be grateful that I finally ignored the feeling, stuffed my fear and anxiety back down inside, and took my first step.

Victory from the Jaws of Defeat

In retrospect I don't think I could have felt the exhilaration and fulfillment of completing my Camino if I hadn't experienced that failure back in 2015. Perhaps the experience of failure is necessary if you want to really grasp the sweetness and significance of success. And I know I'm not the only one who thinks this.

In addition to the Nebraska Cornhuskers, I'm also a big fan of the University of Virginia (UVA) Cavaliers. Nebraska is my home state, so I'll always pull for Big Red, but UVA is where I completed my college education, and this part of the country is where I began my professional career and still make my home. I love my Cavaliers. And like all Virginia fans, I was devastated in 2018 when the men's basketball team, which had entered the NCAA Tournament as the top seed, was upset in the first round by the sixteenth-seeded team from the University of Maryland, Baltimore County (UMBC). This was the first time a number-one seed had been defeated by a sixteenth seed since the tournament was expanded to sixty-four teams in 1985. It was a humiliating loss.

As Coach Tony Bennett and his team went back to work the next season, I'm sure that the abrupt and embarrassing ending of the previous season was foremost in their minds. I would guess that such a painful and public failure must have motivated every practice, every drill, every hour of weight training and other conditioning. That seems to have been the case, because the Cavaliers came back the next year and, after completing a tremendous 35-3 season—going 16-2 in the Atlantic Coast Conference—they won the NCAA Tournament to become national champions, defeating a scrappy team from Texas Tech in overtime, 85-77. I can only imagine how sweet that victory tasted, especially after the bitterness of the previous year's loss.

Coach Bennett gave a speech a few days after the championship game in which he made a statement that has since gone viral: "If you learn to use failure, suffering, or adversity right, it will buy you a ticket to a place you couldn't have gone to any other way." After saying this, he pulled from his coat pocket two tickets: one was to the UMBC tournament game that the Cavaliers lost in 2018, and the second was to the national championship game that they won in 2019.

What a great lesson! In one sentence and with one image, Coach Bennett drove home a central truth: Failure can prepare you for success, if you take the time to learn from it. In fact, the coach took it one step further: Failure is essential to success. If you really want to succeed, you have to fail along the way.

In a study of scientific careers, researcher Dashun Wang and his associates analyzed an incredible 776,721 applications for grants from the National Institutes of Health (NIH) received between 1985 and 2015.[9] Then they went even further, looking at the results of forty-six years' worth of venture capital (VC) startups. Finally, and more ominously, they reviewed data surrounding 170,350 terrorist attacks between 1970 and 2017. Wang, an associate professor of management and organizations at the Kellogg School of Management at Northwestern, summarizes the results of the analysis: "Every winner begins as a loser."

The researchers clarify that, contrary to popular belief, what differentiates those who ultimately succeed from those who continue to fail is not sheer persistence. Instead, those who "try and try again" only find success if they actually learn from their failures. "You have to figure out what worked and what didn't, and then focus on what needs to be improved, instead of thrashing around and changing everything," Wang explains.

Those who managed to apply the knowledge gained from their failures found success, and those who just continued blindly trying "something different" did not. The trend proved out in all three databases: for NIH applications, successful applicants averaged 2.03 failures before succeeding; VC startups failed 1.5 times before finding the winning combination; and—tragically—terrorists averaged 3.9 failed attempts before carrying out a successful attack.

If you think about it, you can probably come up with dozens of similar examples, from history and from your own

---

9   Dashun Wang, Benjamin F. Jones, Yang Wang, "Early-Career Setback and Future Career Impact," *Nature Communications*, October 1, 2019, 10(1): 4331, https://www.nature.com/articles/s41467-019-12189-3.

life. Thomas Edison is often quoted as saying, "I didn't fail 1,000 times to invent the light bulb; I successfully discovered 1,000 things that won't work."

Stephen King, one of the world's all-time best selling novelists, had his debut novel *Carrie* rejected thirty times, discouraging him so deeply that he threw the manuscript in the trash. His wife, however, rescued it and encouraged him to keep trying. Millions of readers today are glad he did! Similarly, J. K. Rowling was a single mom living on public assistance when her idea for a book about a boy with magical gifts named Harry Potter was accepted by a publisher. Within five years she was one of the wealthiest women in the world.

Another wealthy and influential woman, Oprah Winfrey, was fired from her first job as a television news anchor in Baltimore. Walt Disney, Bill Gates, Steven Spielberg, Mark Cuban, and Lucille Ball, among many other notables, are on the ever-expanding list of those who refused to accept defeat at the hands of failure.

The common denominator in all these stories—and the many similar stories you may know—is that in each case, the subject refused to be defined by a particular failure. Instead, each of them learned from failure and then kept trying, determined to reach the goal they had set for themselves. Taking that stance, of course, requires resilience and determination, along with a certain amount of personal courage.

Pride Before a Fall

Those of us who have spent any time around the financial markets are familiar with the concept of learning from failure. In fact, as a wealth manager and counselor, I'm able to speak to my clients from personal experience about the importance of thoroughly absorbing the lessons that failure has to offer.

After graduating from college and working for a number of years as a CPA, I became convinced that I wanted to do more than help people and companies see where their money had gone. I became deeply committed to helping them determine how to look forward rather than backward: to help them grow their wealth and make good decisions about the future of their assets.

But when I started my firm, Bernhardt Wealth Management, I was, like many owners of new businesses, not exactly awash with clients. I had access to a number of good investment alternatives, and I was familiar with the principles of diversification, risk tolerance, and other tenets of portfolio design and management. I knew how to help clients assess their goals and priorities, how to guide them toward an accurate picture of their ability to handle risk, and how to advise them in constructing a well-diversified portfolio that matched their needs, temperament, and long-term objectives. But because the investment advising profession is one that is ultimately built on trust, it took a while before my fee-only wealth management business reached critical mass and became self-sustaining.

In the meantime I was forced to finance my budding enterprise by using personal cash reserves, investments, retirement accounts, lines of credit, and credit cards. Eventually I was leveraged to the hilt.

As if that weren't enough risk, I made a critical error in my personal financial decisions—one I should have certainly known to avoid, since I counseled my clients against it on a regular basis. I decided to trade in my own account, buying and selling some very speculative investments. After all, I knew what I was doing, right? The rules I tried to get my clients to follow—maintain broad diversification, always keep your asset allocation within the parameters of your risk tolerance, avoid decisions made speculatively or on the basis of emotion—didn't really apply to me, did they? When I tripled the size of my account in a short period of time, I was convinced that I was smarter than everybody else in the room.

To paraphrase a biblical proverb: "Pride goes before a fall, and a haughty spirit before destruction." There's a reason this proverb has been around so long: it's true! I learned the truth of it the hard way. By allowing greed to control my investment decisions, I ended up losing $100,000 in my account. And remember, this was at a time when I was financing my business on credit. I certainly didn't have $100,000 I could afford to lose.

I finally decided that I had paid enough tuition at the School of Hard Knocks—an MBA's worth! I had a little meeting with myself and determined that from that point forward, I would follow the same advice I gave my clients. I determined that my personal financial decisions would no longer be driven by any emotion, whether fear or greed. I would stop giving credence to cocktail party talk about "hot" investments and would instead rely upon reliable, evidence-based research.

It was a tough lesson to learn, but the good thing about tough lessons is that they aren't easily forgotten. With time, patience, and perseverance, my business began to turn the corner, and at this writing, we have been in continuous operation for over twenty-seven years. I have been blessed to have talented and committed associates join my firm over the years; presently there are ten of us, all focused intently on serving our clients in "The Bernhardt Way." With hindsight I realize that failure in the early days of the firm gave me something invaluable. As Coach Bennett would put it, it bought me a ticket to a place I could never have gone otherwise.

My work as a wealth manager has taught me again and again that the difference between those who succeed in reaching their financial goals and those who fail is often in their willingness to learn from failure. It just stands to reason that the difference in results must be located in the responses and decisions of each individual; after all, they are all investing in the same financial marketplace. But those who refuse to heed wise counsel or pay attention to empirical research will tend to make the same mistakes and receive the same less-than-satisfactory results, while those who are willing to learn and take good advice will ultimately achieve their goals. Both types of people will suffer setbacks—the markets don't always go up! One group, however, will reach their objectives in most cases, and the other will not.

Learning from Past Failures

As I wrote the initial drafts of this book, financial markets around the world were in turmoil because of the emergence of the COVID-19 virus. This pandemic outbreak, having spread to every continent except Antarctica, had the appearance of a "black swan event"—something never before seen that has unexpected and widespread consequences. As governments rushed to contain the disease, great confusion resulted for investors and analysts who were trying to anticipate the length and breadth of the economic disruption likely to result from attempts to get this pandemic under control.

Markets tend to become volatile in the face of uncertainty, and the COVID-19 outbreak was no exception. When markets become volatile, it is also an opportunity to observe investor behavior at its most basic. Those who have learned the lessons of past failures and have availed themselves of solid advice tend to react one way, and those who have not learned or heeded similar lessons react a different way.

The principal weakness of those who have not learned from past failures is their heightened tendency to fall victim to certain behavioral biases that often come to the fore during times of increased market volatility. The first of these is *herd mentality*, which is what happens to us when we see a market movement afoot and conclude that we had best join the stampede. The herd may be hurtling toward what seems like a hot buying opportunity, such as a run on a stock or stock market sector—think of the dot-com bubble of the late 1990s. Or it may be fleeing a widely perceived risk, such as a country in economic turmoil—or a disruption caused by a pandemic. Either way, following the herd typically puts investors on a dangerous path toward buying high, selling low, and incurring unnecessary expenses en route.

A second behavioral bias that investors must confront in a volatile market is the tendency toward *loss aversion*. As humans, most of us are endowed with an oversized dose of loss aversion, which means we are significantly more pained by the thought of losing wealth than we are excited by the prospect of gaining it. As Jason Zweig, author of *Your Money and Your Brain*, states, "Doing anything—or even thinking about doing anything—that could lead to an inescapable loss is extremely painful."

One way that loss aversion plays out is when investors prefer to sit in cash or bonds during bear markets or even when stocks are going up, but a correction seems overdue. The evidence clearly demonstrates that they are likely to end up with higher long-term returns by at least staying put, if not bulking up on stocks while they are "cheap." And yet even the *potential* for future loss can be a more compelling emotional stimulus than the *likelihood* of long-term returns.

Finally, especially in volatile markets, investors are apt to succumb to *confirmation bias*. This is the tendency to favor evidence that supports our beliefs and gloss over that which refutes them. We'll notice and watch news shows that support our belief structure; we'll skip over those that would require us to radically change our views if we are proven wrong. Of all the behavioral biases on this and other lists, confirmation bias may be the greatest reason why it is important for investors who really want to learn from their past mistakes to avail themselves of solid, research-based advice. Without it, our minds want us to be right so badly that they will rig the game for us—against our best interests as investors.

All of these behaviors come into their clearest view in a bear market. You see, it's much easier to remain calm when prices are going up. But when investors see their value shrinking before their very eyes, emotions kick into high gear. The same impulses that told our hunter-gatherer ancestors to run or get ready to fight for survival are telling us we have to do something before our investments vanish completely. The problem is that the impulses that served our ancient ancestors well in struggles with actual bears are of little use in the bear markets of the modern financial marketplace. Rather than adrenaline-driven action, what is most often called for is calm, logical thought.

For those who have learned the lessons of past bear markets and wild price swings, it is easier to control the impulses to sell everything or buy at any price. But those who insist on following the directions of their emotions are in great danger of doing themselves long-term financial harm. The difference really is in how one responds to the lessons of past mistakes and failings.

BEWARE THESE BEHAVIORAL INVESTING TRAPS

1. Herd Mentality: The tendency to do what "everybody else" is doing. Hint: in the financial markets, the herd is typically wrong.

2. Loss Aversion: When fear of losing money is stronger than anticipation of making money. This causes us to see the glass as half-empty 100 percent of the time.

3. Confirmation Bias: When you only believe information that agrees with your prior opinion. If you live your life in an echo chamber, you miss out on lots of important—if uncomfortable—truths.

"The Next Right Thing"

In many ways my rural and agricultural upbringing on a farm in Nebraska prepared me emotionally for working in the financial services industry. As strange as it may sound at first, farmers and ranchers have a lot in common with wealth managers and financial advisors.

Think about all the things that can happen on a farm or ranch that are beyond the control of the owner: drought, crop-damaging storms, floods, plant or animal disease, not to mention the vagaries of market pricing for agricultural products or the ebb and flow of government policies that impact the agricultural industry. So many circumstances that can directly affect a farmer's livelihood come from places that the farmer can do absolutely nothing about. So what does he do?

He does what my dad did: he concentrates on the things he can control. He takes the best care possible of his equipment and livestock. He rotates crops and grazing patterns to maximize the health of the land. He carefully reviews his operating budget to make sure he's getting the most from every dollar he spends. Rather than reacting in panic, he focuses on each day as it comes. He considers past experiences and applies lessons learned to present decisions. As author Emily P. Freeman advocates in her book, *The Next Right Thing,* he works hard to do exactly what the book title suggests: the next right thing.

In the same way, especially during times of market volatility or uncertainties imposed by pending changes in tax or financial regulations, we counsel our clients to remain calm and logical—to focus on the things they can control. We remind them of previous market cycles and lessons learned there. We help them build diversified portfolios that are not overexposed to risk in any single sector. We rebalance holdings to stay aligned with the client's long-term strategy and goals. We view their situations in light of potential regulatory changes and develop contingency plans.

In other words, we focus on what we can control, and we never forget what previous experiences have taught us about how markets behave. When we're able to help clients see the bigger picture in this way, we are typically able to help them weather the storms and emerge on the other side, poised for future opportunities.

It also helps immeasurably, as I mentioned early in this book, to have trustworthy and encouraging companions for the journey. Julia, from Munich, with whom I struck up a conversation early on my first day of the walk, was my first source of face-to-face encouragement on the Camino. Astrid, Petra, Philipp, Szandra, and Tanja—the members of my Fellowship—offered me, in addition to their friendship, a certain type of accountability to "stay on mission" as we journeyed together—and certainly not in any burdensome, guilt-laden way. Rather, we enjoyed being in each other's company as we each made our way toward a common destination. That made the journey not only more fulfilling, but a whole lot more fun, too.

At my firm, we aspire to offer that same type of encouragement to our clients. We don't see ourselves as financial taskmasters, tut-tutting each time someone strays from the monthly budget or makes a purchase we didn't recommend. Rather, we want to be friendly, knowledgeable guides, enjoyable traveling companions whose only interest is to help our clients arrive at their intended destination. We believe—and this belief was confirmed over and over for me on my Camino pilgrimage—that the best way to help people turn past failures into opportunities for success is to walk beside them, giving them meaningful assistance when needed, and providing encouragement to continue applying the lessons learned as they continue their own pilgrimage.

Learning from Those Who Went Before

The interesting thing about learning from failure is that we aren't limited to learning from our own failures. An adage attributable to many noteworthy people says, "A smart person learns from their own mistakes; a truly wise person learns from the mistakes of others." When you think about it, much of modern science rests on a foundation of learning from others' mistakes. Researchers form hypotheses and test them via experiments. Sometimes those experiments prove the hypothesis to be in error. But even that error provides a clue for building the next hypothesis.

In much the same way, peregrinos on the Camino de Santiago depend on predecessors to leave behind clues that mark the way. In the very earliest days, the best or shortest route to Santiago de Compostela was unknown to most pilgrims. Someone had to begin leaving markers and signs along the way that would benefit those who came after.

As I walked the Camino and followed those signs, I reflected on how important it is to have predecessors and pioneers who are willing to blaze a trail for the rest of us. I hope you'll join me in that reflection by turning to the next chapter.

....

For Reflection

- Have you experienced failures? What, if anything, did you learn from them?

- Are there people you admire who have overcome failure? What do you admire most about them?

....

Scan to see a color image of the photo in this chapter.

CHAPTER 8

Arrows and Seashells

On July 27, 2018, I walked 22.16 miles (almost thirty-six kilometers) as I traveled the Camino de Santiago from Logroño to Nájera. Unfortunately for me, that was about two miles more than I really needed to walk. You see, I was walking with Vicente, a peregrino from Madrid, and I got so engrossed in our conversation that I missed a waymarker. Apparently Vicente wasn't paying any more attention than I was, because he missed it, too.

I might have taken a warning from Brierley's travel guide, which has this to say about this stage of the Camino as one is leaving Logroño: "...with ongoing road improvements, waymarking may be disturbed, so stay fully focused or you might lose your way." Sure enough, this particular day was the most challenging of all for finding the waysigns that all pilgrims depend on in order to stay on the path. On previous days, finding the markers seemed pretty easy, but on this day it was much more difficult, and Vicente and I paid the price for our lapse of attention.

Fortunately for modern peregrinos, the majority of the Camino is abundantly and clearly marked. The two principal

forms of waymarking are the scallop shell that symbolizes the
Camino and yellow arrows, which can be found on a wide variety of surfaces: rock walls beside the roadway, sides of buildings, traffic signs, or on the bases of pilgrim statues such as the
one I passed on July 27 as I was walking my extra-long route
from Logroño to Nájera. In fact, sometimes you can find yellow
arrows painted on abandoned vehicles or farm equipment.

A pilgrim monument outside of Ventosa.

The scallop shell waymarkers take several forms. Many
are rather traditional re-creations of shells, while others are
more stylized. They can appear on the pavement at a pilgrim's
feet, on walls, on stone markers, affixed to bridge railings, or
even incorporated into the ornamental metalwork on gates
and fences. They are also often seen in combination with the
yellow arrows.

I mentioned the origins of the scallop shell as a symbol of the Camino in Chapter 2. The yellow arrows have a more recent origin story. Don Elías Valiña Sampedro, a parish priest in the tiny village of O Cebreiro—located about 160 kilometers east of Santiago de Compostela—was a dedicated student of the Camino de Santiago and its history. Don Elías, born in 1929, even wrote his doctoral thesis on the topic for his studies at the University of Salamanca.

By Don Elías's time, the Camino was known in a historical sense, though it had been mostly forgotten by all but a few exceptionally loyal pilgrims and church historians. His years of study and research convinced him that the Camino was important enough to preserve and even revive, if possible. Don Elías, however, decided to do what he could to bring the Camino back to the prominence he believed it deserved.

He had the idea of marking the French Way, starting in Saint-Jean-Pied-de-Port and continuing all the way to Santiago de Compostela. His nephew relates that on a trip to France, Don Elías noticed many of the signposts for the mountain roads were painted yellow, so he used the same color for his project. Other sources say that road workers who were friends of Don Elías provided him with leftover yellow paint from a construction project. It is said that he loaded his aging Citroën sedan with buckets of yellow paint and, starting from Saint-Jean-Pied-de-Port, drove the whole of the Camino Francés across northern Spain, painting yellow arrows every two kilometers along the way. The story is told that when questioned by curious bystanders or local officials as he painted his yellow arrows, Don Elías would explain that he was "planning an invasion." That would be accurate—though it was to be an invasion that came one, two, or three persons at a time! The total number of Don Elías's "invaders" is now well into the millions.

But Don Elías didn't limit his efforts to what he could do by himself. He was also instrumental in forming various groups and associations to support the repopularization of the Camino de Santiago. He traveled widely, lecturing at universities and conferences across Europe in order to promote and explain the importance of the pilgrimage route and its role in promoting greater understanding among people of all nations. The groups he founded continue to carry out restoration projects on many stretches of the ancient path lost to time and disuse.

Don Elías died in 1989, but his legacy is secure. A bronze bust of the tireless priest overlooks the square of the twelfth-century Church of Santa María la Real in O Cebreiro, where Don Elías Valiña Sampedro is buried; his memory will be revered as long as peregrinos walk the Camino.

Today, the yellow arrow waymarkers are synonymous with the Camino de Santiago and the pilgrims who traverse it. It would be impossible to overestimate the value of these signs along the way. If only Vicente and I had been watching more closely for them instead of focusing on our conversation! We could have saved ourselves two miles.

Those Who Lead the Way

As I walked my Camino I found myself reflecting on the importance of those who have gone ahead of us to mark the way. One lesson I drew from the unintended two-mile detour I made with Vicente that day was the importance of being present—of paying attention to everything around us in the current moment. Because I didn't, I was unable to benefit from the guidance of predecessors like Don Elías and others who tried to leave a well-marked trail for people like Vicente and me.

A larger lesson of course concerns the importance of learning from those who have preceded us. And this is true not only for someone walking a pilgrimage route, but in so many other areas of life. Those of us who were blessed with parents who cared for us can think back on many conversations that started with words like, "I've been around a little longer than you, and let me tell you..." Especially in our teenage years, these conversations likely provoked a lot of eye-rolling, but I have to admit, some of that advice has actually proven to be pretty accurate as I've gotten older.

I agree with the sentiment attributed to Mark Twain: "When I was a boy of fourteen, my father was so ignorant I could hardly stand to have the old man around. But when I got to be twenty-one, I was astonished at how much he had learned in only seven years!"

If we think carefully about it, we all realize, like Sir Isaac Newton, that we have benefitted from the view obtained by "standing on the shoulders of giants." No matter what our profession or field of interest, we all owe a tremendous debt to the pathfinders who left a marked trail for us to follow.

Sometimes those trail markers come in unexpected forms. One of the funniest moments I had on the Camino was on August 13, 2018, as I was covering the nearly nineteen miles from Villafranca del Bierzo to O Cebreiro, the home of Don Elías. The trail was fairly narrow and well-marked. Honestly it would have been pretty hard to go the wrong way on this particular stretch. And yet someone had the thoughtful idea to leave a very special waymarker in the middle of the trail—it was impossible to miss. Maybe the picture I took will help to explain.

Yep, it's horse droppings. I have to admit I never expected to receive a "sign" made from animal dung. But in this case that's exactly what I got. While I didn't really need the directional support on this part of the trail, the laughter I got from this particular "sign along the way" did me a lot of good that day.

I think it's important, from time to time, for each of us to pause and reflect on those who have helped pave our way—even though we may have never met them personally. In my work as a wealth manager, one of those trailblazers was John C. "Jack" Bogle, the widely known and deeply respected founder of the Vanguard Group, one of the largest mutual fund companies in the world. These days, we take it for granted that ordinary investors—not just the super-wealthy—can access professional and cost-efficient fiduciary services and advice. But in the mid-1950s, when Jack Bogle entered the business, these were considered novel, almost outrageous ideas. Jack Bogle believed that the best investment strategies involved long-term commitment to holdings, avoided speculative in-and-out trading, and required patience through market cycles. He also preached against excessive brokerage fees. In the early days, he was largely derided for many of these beliefs, but Jack didn't care. He stuck to his guns and insisted on doing what he thought was right for investors.

In 1975, Jack started what would be the predecessor of the Vanguard 500 Index Fund: the first market index fund available to the general investing public. These days the concept of "owning the market," or index investing, is well known and accepted, but Jack Bogle was the first to create a model that allowed average investors to take advantage of it. For this and many other reasons, Knut Rostad, in his 2013 book *The Man in the Arena*, hails Jack Bogle as "one of the four investment giants of the twentieth century." Similarly, Paul Samuelson, the 1970 Nobel laureate in economics, gave a speech in 2005 in which he ranked Bogle's launch of the first index fund "along with the invention of the wheel, the alphabet, Gutenberg printing, and wine and cheese: a mutual fund that never made Bogle rich, but elevated the long-term returns of the mutual-fund owners—something new under the sun."

Jack Bogle died on January 16, 2019, at the age of 89. His hometown newspaper, the *Philadelphia Inquirer*, printed this accolade:

> "Jack could have been a multibillionaire on a par with Gates and Buffett," said William Bernstein, an Oregon investment manager and author of twelve books on finance and economic history. Instead, he turned his company into one owned by its mutual funds, and in turn their investors, "that exists to provide its customers the lowest price. He basically chose to forgo an enormous fortune to do something right for millions of people. I don't know any other story like it in American business history."

In the service and advice my firm provides our clients, we seek to model the example of Jack Bogle, a farsighted pioneer in the investment world who cared more about doing what was right for his investors than about making a fortune for himself. Jack is one of those predecessors who has left us a clearly marked trail, and I am deeply grateful for that and for every person in my formative years who modeled doing what was right.

Many other waymarkers, less formal and planned than Don Elías's yellow arrows or the scallop shells, adorn the Camino de Santiago. As I continued my pilgrimage, I came to appreciate these as well, reminding me of all the feet that had trod that path before me, and all those that would follow the trail after me.

I've already mentioned the pilgrim statues, frequent features of the Camino that have been erected along the way over many decades. Many are very traditional representations cast in bronze or chiseled in stone or other traditional mediums. They depict pilgrims making the journey or sometimes resting by the side of the trail.

Other statues are very modern in appearance, while still clearly communicating the central message: "You are on the right path, and many have gone this way before you." As I made my pilgrimage I came to appreciate all of the pilgrim statues, my silent encouragers on the Camino.

I think my favorite pilgrim statue, however, was the one I saw while in León on August 7, 2018. Outside the Hostal de San Marcos—a hotel and chapel occupying a beautiful sixteenth-century structure built as a monastery and headquarters of the

Military Order of Saint James—I came across a bronze figure of a seated peregrino. From its posture and expression, it is obvious that the artist captured the moment in each pilgrim's journey when they have reached the end of the day's travel.

Pilgrim statue outside the Hostal de San Marcos.

The figure's eyes are closed; his head leans back, perhaps in an attitude of prayer at the end of a long day of walking, while also contemplating his pain, soreness, and fatigue. His sandals are slipped off, on the ground beside his feet. Looking at the sandals one can see the clear imprint of the owner's feet; these shoes have carried the pilgrim for many steps!

The topic of footwear reminds me of another interesting kind of waymarker I experienced on the Camino de Santiago. It is customary for peregrinos to leave their walking or hiking shoes behind when they have completed their pilgrimage. The worn-out shoes are a vivid symbol and reminder of those who have finished their journey. In some cases there are even sculptures of abandoned shoes in bronze or stone. Like the statues, the arrows, and the seashells, I came to see the shoes as a kind of message of encouragement to complete my walk.

As you can imagine, a pilgrim's shoes are probably the most critical piece of equipment for the journey. I mentioned in Chapter 7 how important it was for me to find the right shoes that would allow me to walk long distances in comfort. Later on I'll tell another story about my shoes and their ultimate fate. Those walking shoes were crucial to my success in negotiating the Camino de Santiago. The number-one problem that causes pilgrims to abort their walk is blisters, and the best preventative measure is to have well-fitting, comfortable, sturdy shoes and the right kind of socks to keep your feet dry, protected, and in good shape.

All of these circumstances factor into the impact of seeing a pair of shoes left alongside the trail. When a pilgrim leaves her shoes on the Camino, it means she has given an offering of the most important thing in her possession. The pilgrim is saying in effect, "These shoes have carried me to my journey's end. I made it—and you can make it, too."

It's important to have that kind of encouragement when you're trying to finish a long journey—no matter what kind of journey it is. There's a particular image in the New Testament that reminds me of this. It's in the Epistle to the Hebrews, the twelfth chapter: "Therefore, since we are surrounded by such a great cloud of witnesses, let us throw off everything that hinders…and let us run with perseverance the race marked out for us."

The biblical scribe has just listed the names of a large group of people who had lived and died long before, reminding readers of their great accomplishments of faith. And then he imaginatively positions them in the grandstand of a track meet where they are cheering and yelling encouragement to those still on the track, straining toward the finish line of the race.

When I was walking the Camino and I would see a pair of abandoned shoes, I had the sense of those who had gone before me and finished their journey, silently cheering me on as I continued toward my goal. It helped me to remember that others had completed the Camino before me and that others would complete it after me. To know myself as a fellow pilgrim in a long line of pilgrims was a great comfort—even on the days when my feet and legs ached and the next albergue seemed a long way off. Like people cheering alongside the route of a marathon race, that "cloud of witnesses" helped to pull me forward, reminding me that the only way to finish my journey was to take the next step.

Of course everyone who walks the Camino experiences a different journey. As I mentioned at the beginning, though all peregrinos share a common destination, they travel many different routes to arrive there. Even those of us walking together on the Camino Francés did not walk the same path because each of us was a unique individual who brought unique abilities, challenges, goals, and understandings to the pilgrimage. After all, "You walk your own Camino." In the next chapter I want to tell you a little more about what this came to mean to me on my journey in Spain—and my further journey through life.

....

For Reflection

- In your professional or personal life, who are the "pathfinders" you admire most?

- Can you think of people who might view you as a pathfinder?

....

Scan to see a color image of the photos in this chapter.

CHAPTER 9

My Way on the Highway

Those who know me can tell you that I am rarely at a loss for words. I usually have no difficulty completing a thought that I am trying to communicate verbally, whether to just one person or a roomful of listeners. But on a sunny afternoon in the central plaza of Estella, Spain, I realized I was having a hard time getting my words past the emotions that kept clogging my throat.

I had walked just over fifteen miles that day (about twenty-four kilometers), covering the route from Puente la Reina ("Queen's Bridge") to Estella. I had kept my breaks relatively short so that I could reach Estella just after noon, before the intense afternoon heat set in. I found my lodgings for the night and took a refreshing shower before getting a bite of lunch and giving myself a walking tour of the small town.

My plan was to find a good spot to sit and record a video message to all the clients of our firm, Bernhardt Wealth Management (BWM). The next day, July 25, 2018, would mark the twenty-fourth anniversary of the business, and it seemed important to me to send a sincere thank-you to the people who make our business possible—our clients. I've already mentioned that BWM had some rough times, especially in the early days. Now, each day makes me more grateful for the wonderful clients we get to work with, and I'm humbled by the trust they place in us by continuing to allow us to serve them and to manage and guide their investment and wealth management plans.

A beautiful and very old stone wall separates the older part of Estella from the newer section.

I found a nice spot in the plaza and settled in with my phone, ready to record my video message. But as I began I realized strong emotions were welling up in me. What was happening? I had done this sort of thing many times, recording happy birthday videos and other greetings to clients and friends of our firm. But today, for some reason, I kept having to restart my recording and collect myself to keep from tearing up and weeping on camera.

As I reflected on this I realized that this wasn't just any video, and it wasn't just any sunny summer afternoon. I was in this particular place on this particular day because of the marvelous and transforming journey I was on—a journey made possible, in large part, by the people I was trying to thank in the video. Hence all the emotion I was feeling. I began to realize that my Camino pilgrimage and my professional journey with BWM were both bound up in the same thing: a lifelong search for my own unique and fulfilling path through life.

It bears repeating that each of us is on a unique and important journey. Whether you are walking a pilgrimage in Spain or making your way along your chosen career path, you are traveling a route across the landscape of life that is yours, and yours alone. It's up to you to decide how you will make that journey; no one else can decide on your behalf. I'm reminded of the old folk song popularized by Woody Guthrie:

You got to walk that lonesome valley,
You got to walk it by yourself,
Nobody here can walk it for you,
You got to walk it by yourself.

This isn't to say that the entire journey is lonesome. There were certainly many times on the Camino when I was walking alone, but there's a difference between solitude and loneliness.

I've mentioned my Fellowship numerous times. Walking the Camino with each of my *compadres* (companions) was a gift, and it also helped me learn the importance of walking my own path in my own way. Each of us eventually developed a routine that was individually comfortable. Some got up earlier, and some got up later. I typically started walking at six thirty in the morning to cover several miles before stopping for breakfast. The others were younger than me, and they were faster on inclines. However, I typically took less time for meal breaks than they did, because I knew that if I didn't, I wouldn't be able to maintain my intended pace and mileage. That meant that for at least some portion of every day's walk, I wasn't with them; they were either ahead or behind me. But I was walking my Camino, not theirs. "Nobody here can walk it for you."

The road from Zubiri to Pamplona. Some of the members of my Fellowship are walking in front of me.

Before I left for Spain, one of the books I read about the Camino was written by a woman who'd injured her ankle on the trail. She wrote that after the injury, she skipped some of the stages of the Camino so that she could stay on schedule for her flight back home. When I read that, I found myself judging her harshly. If she didn't walk the whole route, then she didn't walk the Camino, I told myself. But somewhere along the way I realized my judgment was misplaced.

As I wrote in my Facebook journal on July 24, 2018, "The bottom line is, she walked the Camino she was meant to walk, and she learned things about herself that she wouldn't have learned had she not been injured and walked the entire distance." She walked *her* Camino, not mine."

Walking my Camino, on the road to Pamplona.

The Importance of Informed Advice

In 2006, I decided to run the Marine Corps Marathon (MCM), which is held each year in the Washington, DC area. Dubbed "The People's Marathon" because it is the largest such event in the world that offers no prize money, the MCM draws tremendous local support and typically includes thousands of runners from all over the world, not least because the route passes some of our nation's most famous landmarks. Also, it's a great feeling as a competitor to be cheered on and encouraged by members of the US Marines and US Marine Reserves lining the route.

I hadn't trained for a long-distance run, but despite that, I decided that completing a marathon meant that you had to run the entire 26.2 miles. I had no coach and I didn't ask for advice from anyone who had successfully completed a marathon, but I thought I knew what finishing a marathon meant, and I was determined to do it the "right" way.

I began to train on my own to prepare and ended up injuring my knee. The most unfortunate part of it was that if I had consulted a coach or an experienced marathon runner, I would have learned that there is no rule against walking part of a marathon, a half-marathon, a 5K, or any other running event. In fact, *Runner's World* columnist Jeff Galloway, Olympic running coach Bobby McGee, and LifeTimeRun.com national training manager Rebekah Mayer are just a few of the experienced long-distance runners and coaches who actually advise runners to adopt a walk-run strategy in their races. Mayer, in fact, completed her very first marathon in the excellent time of three hours and fourteen minutes, even though she walked part of the course. But I knew none of this at the time, and I injured my knee as a result. Sadly, my knee has never been the same.

There are two ways of viewing that experience. One is that I trained for *my* marathon, even though I injured myself during my training. But the other view, and the one I think is more constructive, is that walking *your* walk (or running *your* race) doesn't exclude getting good advice from people who've been there before. This goes back to some of the things I mentioned in the previous chapter about taking advantage of the pioneers and those who have left a trail to follow. Certainly one of the most valuable things I did to prepare for walking the Camino de Santiago was to read everything I could find, not only about the history of the pilgrimage, but the advice and words of wisdom from those who had already completed the journey.

As I mentioned earlier, my reading included valuable guidance about the "inner Camino," the spiritual part of the journey, but also practical counsel about pacing yourself, drinking plenty of water, reducing the weight of your pack, and other important tips for making each day's walk the best it could be. So while I walked *my* Camino, I did it with the help and advice of people whose experience and knowledge provided me with a tremendous advantage, even before I had taken a single step. I learned my lesson from my lack of preparedness for the MCM, as my knee reminds me.

This brings me to one of the most common downfalls I see as a professional investment advisor and wealth manager: failure to seek out or heed informed advice. I grimace when I hear someone say they are only going to invest a certain way because that is how their father, spouse, or neighbor told them they should handle their money. "My grandpa lost everything when the banks closed during the Depression, and I don't do anything that's not government-insured," someone might say.

Or "I don't buy anything long term, and I don't trust the stock market."

While I would never downplay the incredible, long-lasting trauma inflicted on an entire generation by the Great Depression—or the Great Recession or the COVID-19 pandemic—as a professional wealth manager I know that while the past is an important guide, research proves it is also an imperfect one. No economic cycle is ever a perfect mirror image of any other; each has its own unique historical, political, and economic contexts. History may rhyme, as Mark Twain supposedly said, but it doesn't repeat itself word for word. History suggests certain patterns but each occurrence stands on its own and requires its own analysis and response.

In fact, the very best analysis and response, based on dependable, peer-reviewed research, is what I try to provide for my clients. For example, one important and often overlooked difference between today's financial markets and those of the 1930s is that during the latter, some 70 percent of the daily volume of buying and selling was generated by individual investors. Today, more than 90 percent of daily volume comes from institutions. Another difference is that central banks, with their monitoring and influence over interest rates and monetary supply, are a prominent feature of today's economic landscape. But in the 1930s, central banks around the world were either slow to react or failed to act at all, leading to a monetary crisis that compounded the effects of the plunging stock market.

While economists still argue over the degree to which more effective central bank intervention could have prevented or lessened the impact of the Great Depression, it is certain that monetary policy, often closely coordinated among the central banks of the deeply interconnected global economy, is now at the epicenter of any response to an economic downturn. Finally, the speed with which today's computer-driven financial markets react to the 24/7 internet news cycle is far beyond anything that could have been imagined in the days of ticker tape and telegrams.

A useful analogy from my experience on the Camino would be the importance of using the most accurate, up-to-date maps available to plan each day's walk. It would be absurd for any peregrino to insist, "I will only use maps that were created in the 1930s; they've been around a lot longer and are therefore the most reliable." As patently unreasonable as this attitude seems in the context of the Camino de Santiago, I still run into folks who carry that logic into their investment decisions.

In other words, we don't live in our grandparents' world, and we aren't navigating their economic or financial landscape. We need to learn from them, certainly, but the answers to our questions are almost certain to be different than theirs. As an investor, you need to "walk your own Camino." You need to evaluate the world you live in and make your decisions based on the best data available, taking into consideration your unique goals, priorities, and preferences.

The majority of the work we do for our clients at Bernhardt Wealth Management consists of helping them thoroughly understand the all-important factors of their goals, priorities, and preferences. Once they get clarity there, we leverage the best, most up-to-date financial research to help them make decisions that support those factors.

Many of our clients are already financially independent individuals with a deep desire to fund or establish organizations that can carry on meaningful work of personal importance to them, even beyond their deaths. For these people, "walking their Camino" means developing strategies to securely fund their philanthropic interests, whether that means getting access to state-of-the-art estate planning counsel, or assistance with setting up an effective board structure to oversee their organization according to their own vision. Our clients depend on us not only to advise and direct their investment and wealth management plan, but also to help them, when necessary, open relationships with the best and wisest minds in areas of expertise necessary to execute their strategies. Our aim is to be the best possible traveling partner, encouraging and assisting where needed in order to free our clients up to spend time on what is most important to them.

Some of our clients are responsible for managing family trusts or foundations: conserving, stewarding, and growing wealth for the benefit of future generations. Our journey with these clients involves staying abreast of current trends in inheritance law and best practices for foundation governance and succession planning. In addition to providing access and recommendations for appropriate investments, we aim to act as a gateway for our clients to the conferences, seminars, and other resources they need to remain confident and knowledgeable in their guidance and leadership.

Small business owners are another vital constituency we serve at BWM. By advising and connecting our clients with the best available resources for retirement plan management, control of capital, and other matters, we seek to become their personal chief financial officer, making more of their time available for big-picture planning and interacting with the people who are most important in their businesses and personal lives.

In all of our client interactions, we seek to embody tenets of The Bernhardt Way, and perhaps most importantly, Principle #19: Invest in Relationships. Indeed, the work we do for our clients is conducted through our proprietary framework we call the Personal Legacy Roadmap^{SM}. Each of our clients is on a unique financial journey based upon their distinct goals, values, and concerns, as well as the legacy they want to create.

We therefore view the time we spend with each client as a vital and necessary investment in our relationship. What we learn and agree upon during this framework guides every interaction with every client. Until we have learned everything we possibly can about them, we aren't in a position to help them walk *their* Camino. Only after we have listened, asked follow-up questions, gained clarity, and reached agreement on priorities with a client are we able to become the reliable and dependable traveling companion we aspire to be. Our investment of time, research, and resources in client relationships is central to our success and, more importantly, the success of our clients.

While every peregrino must walk their own Camino, none of us could make the journey without dependable advice, contemporary maps, and the encouragement of reliable traveling companions.

Even when we have all these things going for us, however, unexpected things still happen. I certainly found this to be true on my Camino. Though I spent considerable time and care in planning, securing the right equipment, and researching the route as thoroughly as possible, my preparation couldn't possibly take into account every event that occurred along the way. The same was true for members of my Fellowship and for every other pilgrim who has ever trod the Camino de Santiago.

This same uncertainty is true of every human journey or undertaking of any kind. To put it politely, stuff happens. Often, how we deal with the unexpected is the most important indicator of success or failure in whatever we are trying to do. In the next chapter I'll tell you about an unexpected thing that happened on my Camino and how I dealt with the challenge and inconvenience—along with the important lessons I gained as a result.

PERSONAL LEGACY ROADMAP: THREE KEY PRINCIPLES

1. Goals: We listen generously to discover what you want to accomplish, what keeps you up at night, and what legacy you want to create.

2. Growth: Each person's journey is different. We create an investment plan to grow and protect your wealth, and to provide the desired income to do the things you want to do.

3. Guidance: Along your journey, we are committed to being your trusted and dependable travel companion, optimizing the possibilities and navigating the detours. In addition to investment planning, we encompass wealth enhancement, wealth protection, wealth transfer, charitable giving, and a broad range of considerations to fully develop your portfolio and allow you to focus on what matters most to you—your family, your business/career, and the causes that matter most to you.

For Reflection

- What is the difference between learning from the past and being bound by it?

- As you think about your unique path, either personally or professionally, how does it differ from that of other individuals in your acquaintance?

Scan to see a color image of the photos in this chapter.

CHAPTER 10

The Day the Bubble Burst

On July 28, 2018, I was finishing my day's walk, having covered the nearly fourteen miles from Nájera to Santo Domingo de la Calzada, when I felt something happen in the heel of my right shoe. A plastic bubble, built into the heel to provide shock absorption while walking, burst. I felt the pop, and with each step I took after that, I could hear air rushing in and out of the bubble.

Knowing that one of my shoes wasn't working the way it was designed was not a welcome thought, as I was still many miles from my final destination and worrying about my shoe would not be a helpful use of my time or mental energy. In Chapter 7, I described my failed attempt at walking the entire length of the C&O Canal, and the painful lesson that taught me about choosing the right walking shoes. As you may recall, I chose my shoes for the Camino after a lengthy process of trying many different pairs before I finally settled on shoes with a shock-absorbing bubble that would carry me along my journey. And now the bubble had burst.

As I wrote in my Facebook journal for that day, "The last thing I want to do is switch shoes now." In fact, there was virtually no chance at all in the middle of northern Spain that I would be able to find a replacement pair to meet my needs and allow me to finish my Camino successfully.

I decided that the best thing to do was just keep going. Maybe the burst bubble wouldn't create any other problems, but if it did, I resolved to deal with them as they came up.

As it turned out, I would face additional issues because of the burst bubble. By the time another two weeks had passed, I had begun noticing a lot of dirt in my right shoe by the end of the day. This meant that the bottoms of my feet were experiencing friction from the soil in my shoe, and I was developing more blisters than earlier in the journey. Blisters are a hiker's nemesis. Only a week or so earlier, I had been saddened to learn upon reaching León that Gary from Rochester, New York, who was hiking the Camino with his son, had been sent home after a doctor told him the infected blisters on his feet would not permit him to continue the pilgrimage.

By the time I reached Sarria on August 15, I had noticed that I could stick my finger from the heel of my shoe all the way inside to where the burst bubble should have been. The hole was letting in trail dirt, and it was creating blisters. Clearly I needed to do something, but I wasn't sure what options I had.

In the spirit of "Phone a Friend" from the hit TV show *Who Wants to Be a Millionaire?*, I decided to pose my problem to friends on social media and ask for suggested solutions. In my Facebook journal for August 15, I posed five possible remedies for my problem and asked for input:

Do nothing. I am four days from Santiago, and if I wrap my foot sufficiently, I will probably be okay. Of course, there is the risk the blister could get infected if it bursts.

Get a new pair of shoes. The risk here is that it took seven pairs to find a shoe that didn't create more blisters. A new shoe could be worse.

Find some duct tape. Certainly one of the 1,001 uses for duct tape must be to tape shoes. But how would I tape the shoe without the tape falling off after a short distance? Maybe I would tape my foot and shoe together.

Find a bag and put my foot in the bag to keep the foot and dirt separated. But my foot may not be able to breathe in that bag.

Walk in my sandals. I walk around with them in the afternoon and evenings. But they might create blisters in other areas, and I don't think I can walk as fast in them.

Other. Any suggestions you have would be appreciated…

Ultimately, I chose Option 3. I was unable to find duct tape in Sarria due to all the stores being closed on Sunday, but I bought a roll in Portomarín, the next major town on my route, after walking an additional fourteen miles, mostly uphill. I was able to hit on a method for taping the heels of both shoes to seal out most of the dirt from the trail and also provide enough adhesion to last a while. Even though I had to retape my shoes every couple of days, I was able to make it to Santiago de Compostela and later to Finisterre in the same shoes I started in.

My shoes after the first day of walking with duct tape.

THE LEGEND OF THE ROOSTER, FROM
SANTO DOMINGO DE LA CALZADA

One of the more charming legends surrounding the Camino de Santiago involves a rooster and a boy falsely accused of theft. The story takes place in the town I entered when the bubble burst in my right shoe: Santo Domingo de la Calzada.

As the tale runs, a pilgrim couple, traveling with their son, stopped at an inn in the town. The innkeeper's daughter was attracted to the son, but he refused her advances. Angry at being spurned, she hid one of her father's silver goblets in the boy's pack, which he unwittingly took with him when the family departed the next morning. The theft was reported, and when the authorities searched the travelers' belongings, they naturally found the goblet. As a result, the hapless boy was taken to the town to be hanged as a thief.

For reasons not made clear in the legend, the parents continued their pilgrimage—presumably lamenting their son's fate and intending to pray to St. James for his rescue. When they returned on their way home, they passed the gallows in the town square of Santo Domingo de la Calzada and saw their son hanging there—and still miraculously alive.

The astounded and delighted parents rushed to the home of the town constable and reported their unbelievable findings. The officer, who was dining on chicken, is said to have told the parents, "Your son is no more alive than this rooster I'm about to eat." At this point, it is said, the erstwhile main course stood up on the constable's plate and began crowing vigorously. The astounded constable ran to the gallows and cut the boy down, giving him a full pardon and restoring him to his parents.

To this day a rooster and hen reside in a cage in the Cathedral of Santo Domingo de la Calzada, a testament to the miraculous survival of the innocent victim. But nothing further is known about the fate of the spiteful girl who falsely accused the young traveler.

The entrance to the cathedral in Santo Domingo de la Calzada. Perhaps the parents of the boy who survived his hanging offered prayers of thanksgiving here. The rooster and hen are caged near the entrance of the church.

Integrity and Bubble Panic

My experience with the burst bubble in the heel of my shoe and my subsequent dilemma about how to salvage my ability to finish my Camino led me along several lines of thought. One that might be somewhat obvious to anyone familiar with the history of the financial markets was about the various "bubbles" that have occurred over the years: instances where prices for a certain commodity or type of investment became driven by buying demand unmoored from reality.

Starting with the "Tulip Mania" of the early 1600s in Holland—when prices for bulbs and exotic hybrids of the newly fashionable flower became ridiculously inflated—and continuing through the well-known "dot-com bubble" of the early 2000s, there have been numerous times when emotionally driven buying pushed prices to levels that had little to do with the actual value of the things being purchased. The dot-com bubble, for instance, became known as such because at that time, in the heady early days of internet commerce, it seemed all one needed to do was announce the launch of a business with "dot-com" as part of the name, and investors would readily pour funds into the enterprise—in many cases without full awareness of how the fledgling company actually made money.

The tendency of investors to allow emotion to drive decisions—whether enthusiasm over the latest "big thing" or unreasoning panic at the thought of the next market crash—is one of the most common habits we seek to counteract as we counsel and advise our clients, as I've mentioned several times. As long as there are markets in which human beings invest, there will be bubbles, and at some point each of them will burst. When we accept this premise ahead of time, we're better prepared to make rational decisions when the time comes.

Another line of thought stimulated by my own personal burst bubble had to do with how easy it is to succumb to fads or gimmicks. These occur in almost every area of life, but the world of finance and investing is especially prone. Those in the business of selling investment products on commission are perhaps the main purveyors of such fads and gimmicks. Friends of mine who have worked at various brokerage houses tell stories of what they call "A-efforts": instances when the parent company had purchased a large block of certain securities or had spent considerable sums developing a particular product and then called upon its sales force to present the "opportunity" to every client. Since the only requirement for firms like this is that the product be "suitable" for the client, it is easy for salespeople to interpret "suitability" pretty broadly—sometimes to the detriment of the client.

In fact, the problem with such an approach is twofold. First, it presumes that the same investment is appropriate—suitable— for every client of the company. This is patently unreasonable since each client is unique—each is in a different stage of life, has a different tolerance for risk, and has dozens of other distinctive factors. Second, it places the emphasis on the benefit to the company—selling a proprietary product—and on the broker or other representative generating a commission, ultimately subordinating the needs of the client to those of the company and the broker.

In our work as fee-only wealth managers, we are legally bound to a fiduciary standard that requires us to make recommendations and provide advice that places the client's interests ahead of everything else. Thus we do not receive commissions on the products or services we recommend. If we did receive a fee or commission in connection with our services or advising, it would need to be fully disclosed in writing prior to the client entering into the transaction or relationship. This standard also means that we have eliminated A-effort-type investment pitches or products built on exotic, complicated financial instruments.

Now I'm not saying that the REI employee who sold me the shoes with the shock-absorbing bubble in the heel was pushing something inappropriate; he was simply sharing a feature Brooks emphasized. I was the person who decided on these particular shoes after trying other pairs and determining that these were the best and most comfortable fit for the amount of walking I planned to do. The principle of the bubble in the heel made sense to me, partly because I had actually tried the shoes and determined they would meet my needs.

But in the investment world, it happens too often that investors are sold products they don't fully understand and have no prior experience with. The typical result is performance that fails to meet expectations—either because the expectations were overblown by an effective sales pitch, or because the investor never really comprehended what they were buying and what the outcomes would be under various scenarios.

At Bernhardt Wealth Management, because we are bound to the fiduciary standard, our chief aim is to make sure not only that we place our client's best interest foremost, but also that our clients understand what we are recommending and why we believe it is in their best interest. We must go beyond mere "suitability." We must fit our actions and recommendations to what is absolutely best for the client.

One reason I feel so strongly about this is that behavioral integrity was modeled for me by my father. As I mentioned in Chapter 4, when he borrowed a shovel or some other tool, he not only returned the tool to its owner, he cleaned it, scraped off the rust, and repaired or sharpened it as necessary. I interpret my father's behavior as "fiduciary": he intended that the tool would go back to its owner in a condition that was in the owner's best interest. Sure, he could have taken a rusted, mud-caked shovel back to his neighbor; that might have been "suitable." But by going beyond what was merely required, my father demonstrated a level of care that prioritized the other person. In my mind, this is what we do when we exercise fiduciary care for our clients.

Expect the Unexpected

Many times during the journey of life, we have to deal with unexpected events. For me on the Camino de Santiago, that meant keeping my shoe functional until I reached the end of my walk.

For our wealth management clients, the unexpected can take a decidedly more unpleasant and complicated shape, such as the sudden death of a loved one or vital business partner, health complications that generate unforeseen medical expenses or force early retirement, or sudden market gyrations stimulated by forces no one could have anticipated—a worldwide pandemic, for example.

One of the reasons we help clients construct well-designed, well-diversified portfolios is to account for as much of the unexpected as possible. By carefully designing an investment plan around each client's risk tolerance, stage in life, and most important priorities and goals, we are attempting to maximize the client's chances to not only survive the unexpected but be able to thrive.

Of course we can only do so much. Sometimes the most useful thing we can do when dealing with the unexpected is to learn what it has to teach us. I learned that shoes can be repaired—for a time, at least—with duct tape. I learned that it's important to keep dust and dirt out of your shoes if you want to avoid blisters.

In the market tumble of 2008, we learned (again) that bubbles always burst at some point. That time it was a bubble created by excess speculation in high-risk mortgages. During the roller-coaster days of spring 2020, we were reminded that black swan events, like a worldwide pandemic caused by a rapidly spreading virus, can bring a sudden end to what many thought was a perpetual bull market.

Each of these lessons, though unpleasant at the time, can be construed as opportunities. In fact, this was another way that my Camino experience reinforced my belief that everything that happens to us—well, almost everything—can be a gift, if we view it the right way. The dust in my shoes coming up through the perforated heel was a gift, because it was a part of my Camino experience and forced me to become creative about ways I could continue my journey.

A setback in business can be a gift if it teaches you something important that you can use as a starting place for even greater successes. An illness or accident can be a gift if it gives you clarity about what is really important in life. Dealing with the unexpected, in other words, can provide you with perspective, experience, and wisdom that you can't gain any other way.

But not all gifts need to come from the unexpected or the unpleasant. Each day, most of us have the opportunity to give gifts both large and small to the people in our lives. The importance of giving back to others is one aspect of life that was reinforced for me almost daily on the Camino de Santiago. The lesson typically came at times when I was least expecting it, as I'll recount in the next chapter.

Buildings in the village of Cirueña, on the way from Nájera to Santo Domingo de Calzada, where the bubble in my heel burst. These buildings are mostly empty, casualties of Spain's "housing bubble." Cirueña is in danger of becoming a ghost town.

....

For Reflection

- What are some "fads" that seemed important at the time but are no longer part of your life?

- How do you judge whether a trend is likely to have ongoing importance?

....

Scan to see a color image of the photos in this chapter.

CHAPTER 11

Busing My Own Table

As you can imagine, food for each day is a principal concern of every peregrino on the Camino de Santiago. People in the towns and villages along the route know this of course, and in addition to the usual cafés and restaurants, there are many small, informal stalls—almost like the sidewalk lemonade stands many of you set up as kids—offering simple fruits, melons, cheeses, and other fare for pilgrims. Some of these places have established prices, and others are "pay what you can" affairs, mainly intended to display goodwill and concern for the thousands who travel the Camino each year.

As I've mentioned, my practice was to get up early, typically before sunrise, and start my walk for the day. After going seven to ten miles, I liked to stop in a village or town and have breakfast. Most restaurants and cafés along the route offer what they call a "pilgrim menu," which generally features two or three choices with a combination of meat, some type of pasta, and a simple dessert for lunch or dinner.

On the morning of July 29, 2018, I stopped in a similar small place for my breakfast. Often these little cafés are strictly mom-and-pop operations with one or both of the owners pre-paring food, serving guests, clearing tables, and washing dishes. As you can imagine, it can get pretty busy. This particular place was like that, with a few tables and chairs scattered along the sidewalk outside, and a very busy señora attending to everything that had to be done.

One of the informal food and drink stands along the Camino.
This one, in San Juan de Ortega, offered simple food and drink in
exchange for a donation. They also offered free massages in the red van
in the picture, but I passed on that opportunity.

I was in the habit, whenever I finished a meal, of gathering up my plate, cup, and utensils, and carrying them to the serving counter or kitchen. It was no trouble for me, and I believed it would save a little time for the busy folks operating the establish-ment. On this morning, when I finished my meal, I did my usual routine and bused my own table. Naturally I had no expectation of any recognition; it was just my way to help out—giving back a little to those who had provided my food.

But the overworked woman at this café noticed, and she was clearly grateful. She gave me a huge smile and said, "Muchas gracias!" over and over again. I was only too happy to help out, but it also gave me a nice boost for the day, pleased that I had made my host's day a little easier. I suppose that in some way, my simple act of service was also a gift to myself for that day.

It also reminded me of Fundamental #25 of The Bernhardt Way:

> Give back. Pay it forward. Regularly seek opportunities to assist those in need. Express genuine gratitude for the help received by paying it forward and helping others. Be a servant leader and put the needs of others ahead of your own.

For me, carrying my dishes back to the kitchen was no big deal. But for the woman running the café, it was a small gift—something to make her morning a bit easier. Not only that, but it made my steps a little lighter. I think that most of the time, when we take a little extra time and trouble to help someone else, we are benefited too. Perhaps it's because we are reminded that all of us are fellow pilgrims on the journey of life, and by helping each other, we are also helping ourselves.

Giving Back

One of the greatest privileges of our work as wealth managers is the opportunity to help our clients realize a philanthropic goal or vision. Through the years, we have facilitated trusts, foundations, and other organizational structures for clients with the strong priority of giving back to society in some meaningful way, utilizing the wealth they have accumulated. Through our professional network of estate planners, legal specialists, taxation experts, and others, we have been able to assist individuals and families with a deep and abiding desire to make a real, lasting difference in the lives of others.

Often the most enriching part of work with our clients is not even strictly financial in nature. Indeed, one of our most important roles, particularly in helping older clients establish philanthropic efforts, revolves around counseling "the next generation." From our position as professional advisors and wealth managers, we can speak knowledgeably about the importance of philanthropy, the responsibilities that go along with wealth, and other important themes needed to nurture a family culture of commitment to a long-term philanthropic strategy.

Preparation of soon-to-be heirs is crucial. According to some estimates, Baby Boomers will transfer something like $68 trillion to their heirs over the next twenty-five years. If that next generation isn't prepared to make good decisions, it's hard to calculate the cost of all the squandered opportunities. For that reason, we help our clients engage in purposeful communication around family philanthropic goals and efforts. Clear communication with adult children about the importance of philanthropy to their aging parents lays the foundation for the next generation of family leaders and their commitment to a philanthropic legacy.

It's important for parents to tell their story to their children in order to convey why charitable causes are so important. For example, a father who had to struggle to gain an education may feel a deep commitment to providing scholarships for academically gifted but financially challenged students. As he tells of his own struggles and his determination to help alleviate the struggles of others, his children gain a deeper empathy, not only for their father, but also for those he desires to help. In this way his values become their values, ensuring that the torch is passed on. Facilitating and guiding conversations like these has provided me with some of the most meaningful experiences I have ever had as a financial professional.

At Bernhardt Wealth Management, this focus on giving back has been one of the most satisfying aspects of our work. Because our goal is to be valuable, reliable "traveling companions" for our clients' financial journey, it is deeply gratifying when we are able to help someone leverage their material blessings to provide untold benefits, perhaps for generations to come. By providing or facilitating the necessary financial management, planning, and other services required, we take significant burdens "off the table" for our clients, affording them the opportunity to relish the joys of providing unselfishly for the needs and dreams of others. And needless to say, by helping them give back in such an important way, we end up receiving more than our share of inner affirmation.

Smiles Are Contagious

About the same time as my experience in the small family café, I came across a sight along the trail that brought a smile to my face, and to those of many of my fellow peregrinos, as well as family and friends who saw it in my Facebook journal and commented on it. Walking beside a wheat field, I noticed a sunflower with a very unusual characteristic: a smiling face.

The "smiling sunflower" on the road from
Santo Domingo de la Calzada to Belorado, July 29, 2018.

I believe it highly unlikely that the sunflower's smile is natural. Maybe the farmer who owns that field plants a lone sunflower near the Camino trail each year, and as the flower approaches full maturity, he plucks a few seeds to form eyes and a smile. I thought it possible that a pilgrim on the trail was responsible. However, a friend who walked the Camino a year or two after I did told me of a dried sunflower head in that area with the remnants of a smile. This leads me to believe that the planting and doctoring of the sunflower is an annual ritual of the farmer's, not the one-off work of a passerby.

Whatever its source, the "happy sunflower" gave me a smile of my own and inspired me to take its picture. In fact, as I shared this image, both with fellow peregrinos who saw it on my phone and those with whom I shared it on social media, I noticed that the most common reactions were a smile, maybe a quick laugh, and a lighthearted moment. This reminded me of another principle of The Bernhardt Way, #26:

> Keep it fun. While our passion for excellence is real, remember that the world has bigger problems than the daily challenges that make up our work. Stuff happens. Keep perspective. Don't take things personally or take yourself too seriously. Laugh every day.

As I wrote in my Facebook journal for this date, "A smile or laughter brings people together and can encourage someone." The enjoyment I got from the sunflower picture was a gift that I have carried with me ever since.

Keeping It Real

Unexpected gifts like the smiling sunflower abounded on my Camino. A day or two before seeing the sunflower, as I was sitting in a small sidewalk café with Frieda from Liverpool, England, I noticed a group of musicians who appeared to be in costume strolling along the busy street. They were playing and singing, giving every appearance of enjoying themselves very much. Their enjoyment was contagious, and Frieda and I, along with everyone in earshot, got a tremendous lift as well. We learned later that they would be performing in the cathedral after mass that evening.

Musicians on the street in Santo Domingo de la Calzada.

Sitting at my table with some fellow pilgrims and hearing the music, sensing the obvious joy of the performers and their listeners, I had an overwhelming sense of receiving a gift. Simply to be present in that moment, to be alive to the sights, the sounds, the taste of my food, and the expressions on the faces of those around me—all of it was a tremendous gift, and, like the best gifts, was completely unplanned and unexpected.

One of the principal lessons in all this for me was reinforcing the importance of "being present," as I mentioned in previous chapters. In many ways, the practice of being present is similar to the concept of mindfulness, well known to those who regularly practice meditation. In fact, a popular mindfulness website (Mindful.org) defines it as "the basic human ability to be fully present, aware of where we are and what we're doing." This is an apt description of how and why the Camino de Santiago became so meaningful to me, and why I made "being present" my central goal.

When you are living an enjoyable moment, it's a shame to not be fully aware of it. To see the smiling sunflower and enjoy the pleasant reactions of my fellow travelers when I shared it with them; to hear the musicians singing; and to see the smiles it brought to the faces of those around me—these were profound gifts, all the more powerful because they could only be experienced in the moment.

After walking the Camino, I am more convinced than ever that the ability to sense, experience, and savor these unexpected, unplanned moments is essential to living a full life. I believe that the people who are best able to "keep it fun"—to laugh at themselves and with others, to recognize the little joys that show up at unexpected times and places—are the same people who are most able to manage the more serious, challenging times in life. "Keeping it fun" may be an essential ingredient of "keeping it real."

On my pilgrimage along the Camino, I met many peregrinos who, it seemed to me, had mastered the art of keeping it real. Walking beside them and having the privilege of learning a little bit of their life stories gave me the chance to gain some of the deepest and most lasting spiritual keepsakes of the entire journey. In the next chapter I want to tell you the story of one of those fellow travelers.

For Reflection

- Do you think it is important to notice the good moments in life? Do you do anything special to make sure you notice or commemorate them?

- What do you do to keep it fun?

Scan to see a color image of the photos in this chapter.

CHAPTER 12

Ole's Walk to Freedom

Ole was seventy years old when I met him. It was August 1, 2018, and we were walking the Camino de Santiago on the stage from Burgos to Hontanas—the first part of the Meseta crossing. I soon learned that he was from Denmark and that this was his fourth time to walk the Camino. And although the time I spent conversing with Ole was brief, it was rich.

Ole told me about his life, about what it was like for him growing up in Denmark. He had served in the military, an experience that taught him about responsibility and learning one's true limits. He walked with a slight limp, but even at age seventy, he still set a pace not everyone could match, especially for an entire day of walking.

He told me that for him the Camino de Santiago represented freedom. "Everything I really need is in my backpack," he said. "When I am hungry, I can stop for some food. At the end of the day, I can find a place to rest for the night. I don't need much else, other than what I can carry. That is true freedom."

That perspective really struck home with me. I had been having many of the same feelings. There is something profoundly clarifying about the simplification that happens on the Camino. Each day is focused on clear goals: reaching the next town, covering the needed distance. Likewise, the needs of a peregrino are basic: enough food to provide energy, enough water to remain hydrated, sturdy footwear to protect against blisters and injuries.

So often in our society, we confuse "wants" with "needs." In financial counseling, we see this pretty often as we work with clients. One of the most important things we can do is to help clients gain clarity about their true priorities. Until they gain that clarity, our ability to help them is rather limited.

I certainly don't mean to indicate that we should all sell everything, load a backpack, and embark on a life of wandering from town to town. After all, when I finished walking my Camino, I came back to a comfortable home, the usual round of appointments, meetings, and all the other work and obligations that come with the life of most professional people in modern society. And we all have responsibilities to others that are a part of living in relationship with other people. Parents have a responsibility to take care of their children, to provide for their health, growth, and education. We have a responsibility to provide for our families and for our own futures, so as to not become dependent on or burden others. Certainly we try to help our clients make smart financial decisions as a part of encouraging good stewardship of the resources they have been given.

But since walking the Camino, my attitude has shifted regarding how I understand my own wants and needs. I think I became more aware of the difference between the two, because if we aren't careful, the "stuff" we have worked to obtain begins to own us, instead of the other way around. Like Ole, I think my Camino experience gave me a different perspective on what constitutes true freedom. Too often we think of freedom in terms of the ability to buy anything we need. But what if true freedom means needing only what we already have?

Ole also told me that almost everyone can do about 15 or 20 percent more than they think they can. He said that when he was in the army, he often felt he was being pushed beyond his limits. "I learned that I could almost always do a little more than I thought I could—and about 100 percent more than my mother thought I could," he said with a chuckle. I learned later that David Goggins, a retired Navy SEAL and author of the best-selling book *Can't Hurt Me*, believes that when we think we have reached our limit, we have actually only reached about 40 percent of our capacity.

Ole's comment about his mother hit home. Although I'm pretty sure my mother believed in me, I know that at various times in my life I've had to find the inner resources to keep going just a little longer than I thought I could. Ole's observation made me wonder about how we might be setting limitations on ourselves that should be reconsidered.

A Wrong Step Averted

One of the most interesting things about the Camino is the way it changes how we think about ourselves and others. When your day is planned around walking from point A to point B, it provides you with more time to listen to your own thoughts—to step back from the frantic activity that characterizes so much of our lives and to occupy a quiet inner space that tends to get drowned out by modern life. I suppose a lot of this goes back to the notion of being present—giving focused attention to each moment as it passes, rather than being distracted by something that has happened or something that might be about to happen.

Being present and attentive to the moment can even keep you healthy. At least, that's how it worked out for me on at least one occasion on my Camino when I was within four days of reaching Santiago de Compostela.

I'd spent the night of August 17, 2018, in the town of Portomarín, and in the early morning, the time when I typically started on my day's walk, the air was foggy, in addition to the predawn darkness. The day before, upon arriving in Portomarín, I had climbed the fifty-two stone steps leading up from an ancient Roman bridge that serves as the main entrance into the town. At the end of a day's walk, that flight of steps can look pretty steep and long. In fact, on a number of online forums for Camino pilgrims or those planning a pilgrimage, you can find questions about the steps up into Portomarín: whether there is another way into the town, how difficult the steps are when it's raining, and other similar comments.

I didn't think much along those lines upon my arrival in Portomarín, but the next morning, when the time came for me to descend the steps and return to the main pilgrimage route, I had cause to consider them much more carefully. You see, as I was setting out on that dim, misty morning, I was focused on other matters, especially trying to locate the trail signs that would get me back to my planned route. And as I slowly walked in the fog while studying my map, I felt my toe go over the edge of the topmost step.

I was able to stop in time, and then I realized where I was. I also realized what the consequences would have been if I had not stopped or if my step was slightly longer. Another nine inches or so, and I would have likely fallen back down the fifty-two steps I had climbed the previous day. A broken shoulder, rib, or leg would have been a very possible outcome, if I was fortunate enough to avoid more serious injury. At the very least, my Camino would have come to a sudden and very unpleasant end, right there at the base of the steps to Portomarín.

The stone steps at Portomarín.

For much of that day as I walked, I pondered the lesson in my near miss with disaster. How much difficulty and trouble could we save ourselves if we paid more attention to our surroundings and focused more on each moment? I tried to remember other times in my life when being distracted and not present in the moment brought me negative consequences. I also wondered if there was any connection between freedom from distraction and the freedom that Ole had talked about as we had walked together.

Certainly when our lives become too cluttered with unnecessary things, it can easily become a source of distraction, making it much more difficult to pay proper attention to each moment as it is lived. And that sort of distraction can have serious consequences, as I realized that morning at Portomarín.

"You Matter"

One of the best moments of my Camino—and I think this must be true for many other peregrinos—had come a few days earlier, as I reached the highest point of elevation on the French Way. By that time I was feeling intensely connected to all the pilgrims of the Camino, past, present, and future; to my own purpose for traveling the pilgrim path; to my joy in being there; and to the actual spirit that animates and motivates the entire principle of the Camino de Santiago. As I reflect on it, it was also a moment of connection to the sense of personal freedom that Ole had talked about and that I was coming to value so deeply as I walked the Camino.

At the high point of the route, a simple, unadorned cross rises beside the pathway. The cross is made of iron and mounted

atop a five-meter wooden pole. It is called the *Cruz de Ferro*—
"The Cross of Iron"—and this modest monument forms a deeply
spiritual highlight for thousands of peregrinos year after year.

It may be surprising to some to realize that the highest
point on the Camino Frances—the French Way—is not on
the passage over the Pyrenees that crosses the border from
Saint-Jean-Pied-de-Port in France and leads to Roncesvalles
in Spain. The highest point of that first leg of the French Way
is 4,719 feet of elevation, but the Cruz de Ferro sits higher,
right at 5,000 feet.

I reached Puerto Irago, where the Cruz de Ferro is located,
on August 10, 2018. The iron cross is said by some to occupy
the site of an ancient Roman shrine to Mercury, the patron
of travelers. Whether that is true or not, it would certainly
make sense for the Romans to place a marker at this strategic
place along what has been a trade route for centuries, perhaps
going all the way back to the native Celtiberians even before
the coming of the Romans.

THE HOLY WRATH OF ST. JAMES

As with many places along the Camino de Santiago, a number
of legends surrounds the Cruz de Ferro. One of these suggests
that the Apostle James himself was traveling the road when
he saw a group of people performing a human sacrifice. Filled
with holy wrath, he threw a stone at the pagan altar, shatter-
ing it to small pieces. The sacrifice thwarted, St. James had
a cross erected to commemorate the power of the Almighty.

The modern pilgrim tradition for the Cruz de Ferro involves placing a small stone or other token at the base of the cross. It is said that travelers should bring a stone from their home, symbolizing worries or burdens they have been carrying. When they place this stone at the foot of the Cruz de Ferro, they can go on their way, free of their burdens and thankful for their deliverance from it.

The stone I left at Cruz de Ferro, beside those left by other pilgrims. Notice the inscription left by an Italian family, "Famiglia Trovato: 10/08/18," which, in the European format, means they arrived on August 10, 2018, the same day I did.

I felt a little conflicted about this tradition because the very act of walking the Camino felt intensely freeing for me. I didn't feel as if I were carrying a particular burden that I needed to lay down. However, about a week before I left for Spain and my Camino, I found the stone you see in the accompanying photograph. Someone had written a positive message on it and left it to be found by others. I noticed it lying beside the curb where I was parked on that particular day as I was running an errand at a local shopping center. The stone certainly brought a smile to my face, but I wondered if carrying it to Cruz de Ferro might be disrespectful in some way, since the inscribed message—"You matter!"—wasn't a burden or worry, but inspiring words. I decided that finding it was somehow a sign and message of its own. It proclaimed something I deeply believe that would be worthwhile to leave for another pilgrim to find.

Stones are not the only mementos pilgrims leave at the base of the Cruz de Ferro. I have heard of service members who leave their dog tags, or those of fallen comrades. I decided to leave a Bernhardt Wealth Management challenge coin.

You may know that various organizations—military, non-profits, corporations, and others—create challenge coins as a memento or recognition of accomplishment for members of their group or other significant people. A while back, I decided to have bronze challenge coins made for Bernhardt Wealth Management. On the front is the name of our firm, with the word "fiduciary," which describes our commitment to serving our clients' needs above our own. On the back side is the image of a piano, encircled by the words, "Character, Chemistry, Caring, Competence": the "Four Cs" of Bernhardt Wealth Management. Why the piano? Well, that is a tribute to my mom, Irene Elizabeth Ann Bernhardt.

The Bernhardt Wealth Management challenge coin.

My mother was born during the depths of the Great Depression on the windswept plains of Nebraska. As a child she showed an aptitude for music and loved nothing more than playing the piano, both at the small Lutheran church she attended and at home where she often held impromptu concerts for family and friends.

When my mom passed away in 2006, I donated a Steinway Model L grand piano to the Alexandria Presbyterian Church in Alexandria, Virginia, in memory of my mother. The image of the piano on the challenge coin reminds me of her and her love for music, her dedication to her family, her enthusiasm for the Nebraska Cornhuskers and the Los Angeles Dodgers, her unshakeable religious faith, and the myriad ways in which she molded me into the person I am today.

Me kneeling at the foot of the iron cross at Cruz de Ferro
during sunrise on August 11, 2018. My friend Tonnie, from the
Netherlands, took this picture for me.

As I walked away from the foot of the Cruz de Ferro, I felt
a tremendous sense of blessing and fulfillment. Like Ole, I was
learning that traveling the Camino can be an intensely freeing

experience, and while I didn't feel that I had left a burden behind at the foot of the cross, I did understand how good it felt to realize that everything I needed was with me in that moment—true freedom.

Life in the Details

One of the most liberating things about simplifying one's life is the extra time provided for appreciation of the many details we miss when we're in a hurry all the time. We've all seen some form of the witticism that one's main interest or hobby—football, quilting, music, coffee—is "life, and the rest is just details." But I've become convinced, as architect Ludwig Mies van der Rohe famously noted, that "God is in the details." When we gloss over the fine-grained elements of each day, our life is diminished; we are diminished.

The truth of this notion came home to me in so many different ways during my pilgrimage along the Camino de Santiago, but there was one day in particular that stands out in my memory. As our journey continues, I'd like to tell you about it.

For Reflection

- In your own life, how would you define "living in the moment"?

- Do you agree or disagree with the statement: "You can always do more than you think you can"?

Scan to see a color image of the photos in this chapter.

CHAPTER 13

Ant Lines

In 2011, psychology researchers at the University of Utah conducted an interesting experiment.[10] They wanted to explore
the phenomenon of "inattention blindness," when people fail to
see or notice something happening right in front of them. This
is the trait often behind negligent drivers who are distracted
by a phone conversation. Even while looking at the road, they
don't register what is happening ahead, such as the brake lights
of the car in front of them.

For their experiment, researchers Janelle Seegmiller, Jason
Watson, and David Strayer re-created a famous video that was
the subject of the 2010 book *The Invisible Gorilla: How Our
Intuitions Deceive Us*, by Christopher Chabris and Daniel
Simons. In the video, two teams of three people pass basketballs
to each other. One of the teams is dressed in white shirts, and
the other team is dressed in black shirts. Viewers are asked to
count how many times the white-shirted team passes the ball.

---

10   University of Utah, "Missing the Gorilla: People Prone to 'Inattention
      Blindness' Have a Lower Working Memory Capacity," *ScienceDaily*, April
      18, 2011, www.sciencedaily.com/releases/2011/04/110418083249.htm.

During the video, a person in a gorilla suit walks into the frame, stands in the middle of the action, pounds his chest, and strolls off. In the version created by Seegmiller and her colleagues, in addition to the gorilla, one of the black-clad players leaves the scene completely, and the backdrop curtain changes color, from red to gold. The researchers noted that about half the subjects to whom they showed the video failed to notice the gorilla at all. A friend of mine who knew about the gorilla beforehand told me that though he saw the gorilla in the video, he nonetheless completely failed to notice either that the black-shirted player left the video or that the curtain changed color.

The upshot is that when we are distracted, we can miss things that should be obvious to us. In the case of distracted driving, this creates a dangerous situation in a hurry. But even when we aren't behind the wheel, distraction can cause us to miss the important things going on all around us.

On August 14, 2018, I walked from the tiny village of O Cebreiro to Triacastela, a distance of about fourteen miles (almost twenty-three kilometers). As I was leaving O Cebreiro, I noticed an interesting contrast: on one side of the trail, a seemingly endless plain of clouds stretched as far as I could see. On just the other side I saw a completely different scene.

The clouds stretched away into the distance from the slope below the trail leading out of O Cebreiro. This also gives you an idea of the elevation of this part of the Camino.

On just the other side of the trail, the view was completely different.

As I walked along, I felt grateful for the opportunity to notice the extreme contrast between these two views, separated by such a short distance (the entire village of O Cebreiro would fit within the boundary lines of an American football field). That realization led me to think about other things I had noticed as I walked the Camino. Here is what I wrote in my Facebook journal for that day:

> For today, I would like to share an observation and some information. First, the information: As you may or may not know, a pilgrim can get a certificate for walking, biking, or horseback riding [on the Camino]. There is a minimum distance one must travel to get the certificate for each of those three. For walking, it is 100 kilometers—a four- or five-day walk.
>
> I have already shared that the 100-kilometer walk would not have been as impactful for me as four weeks of walking with a 20-pound backpack. In my case, [the route will cover] 780 kilometers and more than four weeks with a 22-pound backpack. If someone asked, I would tell them to walk from Saint-Jean-Pied-de-Port, if possible, or from Pamplona to save three days. I think I am still on track to walk into Santiago de Compostela on my thirty-first day of walking.
>
> I have not seen any pilgrims on horseback but I have seen pilgrims on bicycles. And I would still tell an avid biker to walk if possible. One of the reasons is that [unless you walk,] you miss the "little things."

I remember walking and seeing "ant lines" across the road on multiple occasions. I stopped many times just to watch the ants go from one side of the road to the other on this trail they created. It actually gave me joy, and I felt sorry for bikers and horseback riders because they would miss that.

It then made me think about what little things we are overlooking in our daily lives. Is it time with a child, spouse, or significant other? Is it acknowledging someone we pass in the ordinary course of our day? Living in a large city like Washington, DC can feel like a rat race, and it may be easy to overlook little things that can be so very important to us personally or maybe to someone else. Is there a little thing we can do to make the day better for someone we know or meet? Just a thought.

I count myself fortunate to have grown up on a farm, where I was exposed almost daily to the natural world and its fascinating creatures, large and small. Some of the most interesting of those creatures were the tiniest ants. And I'm not alone; people have been interested in ants for thousands of years, as they are even mentioned in the Old Testament. In Proverbs 6:6, you can read these words: "Go to the ant, you sluggard; consider its ways, and be wise! It has no commander, no overseer, or ruler, yet it stores its provisions in summer and gathers its food at harvest." (New International Version)

Now it's not precisely true that ants have no overseers or rulers; each nest has a queen and the worker ants are dedicated to her care and feeding, as she produces the entire population of the colony. But there are other interesting facts about ants that make them worth our time and attention. For instance, did you know that a worker ant will travel as far as one hundred yards from the nest in its search for food for the colony? That's comparable to a human going eight miles on foot. And since ants can carry fifty times their own body weight, that same worker ant can haul back to its nest the equivalent of 8,900 pounds on a human scale.

When an ant goes in search of food, it follows a somewhat meandering path until it locates a food source. But once the source is located, the ant makes a beeline (pardon the pun) back to its colony, leaving behind a trail of pheromones as chemical "breadcrumbs." When it arrives back at the nest, it communicates its find to other worker ants, and they set out toward the food source, following the trail left by the returning worker. As they go, each worker ant leaves additional pheromone markers on the route, creating an unmistakable path for other ants to follow. Before long, the route to and from the food source is an ant superhighway, with hundreds of ants going in both directions as they focus their efforts on fully exploiting the food source on behalf of the colony and its queen.

There are dozens of lessons that could be drawn from observing an ant line. We could think about the importance of contributing to the common good, dedication to important tasks, and the benefits of well-defined roles within an organization. Because I'm a wealth manager, most would probably expect me to use the ant as an example of making disciplined provision for the future, along the lines of the biblical reference above.

But what really impressed me the most from my time observing the ant lines on the Camino de Santiago is simply the importance of noticing—really seeing and comprehending what is right before our eyes. I've already mentioned in several connections that I made my pilgrimage on the Camino with the overarching purpose of being truly and authentically present in each moment. I suppose some might say that when we put ourselves in a foreign country or some other unfamiliar environment and undergo a unique experience, it's somehow easier to be "in the moment," because each moment presents sights, sounds, smells, and sensations we've never encountered before. "Of course you were in the moment, Gordon," they might say. "Everything you saw, touched, and did was new, a first-in-a-lifetime event."

However, I think it's not only possible but vital to cultivate the skill and habit of intentional noticing, every single day, even amid our customary day-to-day routines. And you don't have to be on a trek through Spain to gain the benefits.

When I speak of "intentional noticing," some may be reminded of mindfulness, which is a very popular practice right now. Those who practice mindfulness typically cultivate disciplines of meditation and close attention to what is happening in their bodies—their breathing, their pulse, the tension in their muscles or the lack of it—in order to heighten their awareness of themselves and their place in the world. A growing body of research indicates that such practices can improve physical, emotional, and mental health. Mindfulness practices have been shown to reduce blood pressure, ease feelings of depression, and even improve memory and other cognitive activity.

The type of mindful attention I'm talking about, however, though related to the practice of mindfulness, is slightly different. What I'm referring to is developing the habit of noticing the details of what is happening around us, whether it's ant lines across a footpath or a new barista handing us our coffee at Starbucks. As with meditation, I believe the act of mindful noticing can have a number of positive outcomes, both physically and mentally.

I'm not alone in this belief. Harvard psychologist Ellen Langer's groundbreaking research into the effects of mindful attention in everyday life offers stunning insight into the benefits—spiritual, emotional, and practical—of consciously perceiving the details of our daily experience.[11] Langer, sometimes called "the mother of mindfulness," has been doing research for the past forty or so years on what happens when we really notice our surroundings. "Much of our behavior is mindless," she says, providing an example from a transaction she made at a department store. Langer had forgotten to sign the back of the credit card she was using, and the sales clerk asked her to do so. She signed the card and then handed it to the clerk, who used it to complete the purchase. The clerk handed Langer the receipt for signature, and then she compared the signature on the receipt to the one on the card—which she had witnessed only moments before! In other words, the sales clerk's behavior was rote, unthinking—mindless.

By contrast, Langer urges her readers and audiences to practice what she calls "the art of noticing," which she explains as "the process of actively noticing new things, relinquishing preconceived mindsets, and then acting on the new observations." By doing so, Langer suggests, we can break out of the ruts of

---

11 Alvin Powell, "Ellen Langer's State of Mindfulness." *The Harvard Gazette*, October 1, 2018, https://news.harvard.edu/gazette/story/2018/10/ellen-langer-talks-mindfulness-health/.

well-worn thinking that we all tend to fall into from time to time. Langer believes that "actively noticing new things" continually puts us in the present moment, making us more sensitive to context and perspective, more engaged.

In Chapter 6, while discussing the benefits of taking "the scenic route," I referred to a European study that found those who commuted to work through settings with more natural features scored higher for mental health than those who commuted only through urban areas. I think that is another proof of the power of noticing. And research also indicates that this principle applies to more than trees, meadows, and ant lines; it also applies to noticing the people we interact with, even casually.

Psychologist Susan Pinker's book, *The Village Effect: How Face-to-Face Contact Can Make Us Healthier, Happier, and Smarter*, captures the results of her research in the field of social neuroscience:[12] the study of how our social interactions affect our brains and nervous systems. Pinker's conclusions point to the fact that as humans, we are hardwired to need meaningful interaction with others in order to thrive. And this includes more than just our families and close friends; it also matters that we have more informal interactions, such as with the people we pass on our morning walk or the waitperson serving us lunch.

In fact, Pinker's research indicates that the number-one predictor of a long and healthy life is the quality of what she calls "social integration": the degree to which you interact in person with a variety of people during the course of your day. By "social integration," Pinker is referring to things as simple as saying hello to the checkout clerk at the grocery store, talking to your next-door

---

12   Susan Pinker, *The Village Effect: How Face-to-Face Contact Can Make Us Healthier and Happier* (New York: Vintage Canada, 2015).

neighbor for five minutes about last night's ball game, and exchanging pleasantries with the barista serving your coffee. This includes your closest relationships, but it expands to even brief interactions.

Do you think it would make a difference in your day if you made a conscious decision to really notice the people with whom you interact? Of course, I'm not suggesting that you should stare at the person seated across the aisle at the restaurant or ask deeply personal questions of the parking garage attendant. I'm talking about exchanging sincere pleasantries, wishing someone a good day and really meaning it—taking the time to look another person in the eye, if only in a fleeting encounter, and recognize the humanity we all share.

During the throes of the COVID-19 pandemic, one of the most serious threats to our mental and physical wellbeing was the severe limitation placed on our ability to have these types of face-to-face interactions. In an April 2020 interview with National Public Radio,[13] Pinker stated that the isolation imposed by the pandemic was "a huge problem, because real social contact is a biological need like eating, drinking, or sleeping. And our bodies react to the loss of that interaction the way we react to hunger. It's physically painful. It's damaging. It's even dangerous, long-term."

She went on to say, "We need to see the whites in each other's eyes to know that we trust people. We need to have a slap on the back or a handshake or a hug...So when we're isolated from people, we're missing all of those signals. And they're very, very basic to our evolution as a social species."

---

13 "Susan Pinker: What Makes Social Connection So Vital to Our Well-Being," *TED Radio Hour,* April 24, 2020, https://www.npr.org/2020/04/24/842604367/ susan-pinker-what-makes-social-connection-so-vital-to-our-well-being.

In other words, noticing is part of what makes us human. When we go through our days on autopilot, failing to see the beauty—and even sometimes the ugliness—in the details of life as it happens all around us, we become a little less healthy, a little less kind, a little less satisfied, a little less involved. We become a little less. I don't want to live my life that way. Do you?

It may be that the ability to notice is closely related to the freedom that Ole talked about as we were walking together. When we understand that our true needs are simple and that we lack for nothing that really matters, the resulting freedom of mind may enable us to see more of what is all around us.

In a similar way, this freedom of mind can enable us to look at life and its experiences in a whole new way. I've spoken several times in previous chapters about the gifts that the Camino gave me, and also about the principle I heard from many peregrinos, that everything the Camino gives is a gift. I learned the truth of this principle in some unexpected ways, and in the next chapter, I'll tell you about some of them.

....

For Reflection

- Do you consider yourself a "noticer"? Do you think this is important or unimportant?

- Are you a person who usually makes eye contact with others when in conversation? What are the advantages and disadvantages of doing so?

....

Scan to see a color image of the photos in this chapter.

CHAPTER 14

Everything Is a Gift

I've already shared the story of the problem I encountered with one of my shoes, when the shock-absorbing bubble in the heel of my right shoe burst (Chapter 10). Eventually the burst bubble developed into a hole in my shoe that allowed dust from the trail to get inside, creating friction that would, if ignored, lead to blisters—the number-one threat to anyone who walks the Camino de Santiago.

I shared the unusual perspective I gained from that experience: that even a setback, such as a damaged shoe, can be an opportunity—a gift. I had to figure out how to use duct tape to seal my shoes, and I eventually came to see that whole experience as a positive thing. Here is what I wrote in my Facebook journal on August 17, 2018, when I arrived in Casanova after a 21.76-mile walk from Portomarín:

...[I]t seemed appropriate to share a photo of my shoes. The duct tape worked, although you can see that I will need to tape them every couple of days. Obviously, I have never worn out a pair of shoes so quickly before. If you look closely, you can see that the shoe is bald in parts.

They say everyone's Camino is different, and I believe it. I also look at every adversity on the Camino as a gift. So, my shoes with holes in the sole are a gift. I am trying to find a life lesson from this, but I am grateful for this gift. I really love these shoes and will tape them as many times as necessary to get them through six more days of walking on parts of the Camino and for little walks in communities. They will make it back to the United States with me.

I still feel blessed and very fortunate. This continues to be a great experience in every way. Thanks for your prayers, support, and encouragement.

You can see the photograph that accompanied this entry in Chapter 10. Ultimately, rather than bringing my shoes home with me as I wrote on Facebook, I decided to leave them behind along the trail as a sort of offering. This is something that many peregrinos do, as I mentioned in Chapter 8.

I think that one reason I was able to view the problem with my shoe—which most people would classify as such—as a gift is that I had such an overwhelming sense of gratitude as I walked the Camino. In fact, I often found myself reflecting on that gratitude and wondering why we couldn't bring that same attitude to every single day of our lives.

I have heard of the Jewish rabbinic concept that God keeps a covenant with the world every day, when the sun is permitted to rise. In other words, every day is a promise kept, a blessing granted. That idea makes a lot of sense to me, especially after walking the Camino de Santiago. I think it really is possible to greet each day as a gift waiting to be enjoyed. The logical extension of that idea, then, is that whatever happens during that day is an opportunity to learn, to grow, or to improve in some way—even if that happens to include a hole in a shoe.

I left my shoes at the base of this pilgrim statue in Finisterre, where I ended my pilgrimage.

Another situation that I received as a gift—though I initially thought of it as an annoyance—had to do with my camera. I had purchased it before my trip because of its small size and light weight, thinking that it would enable a visual record of my experience. But I didn't really have time to practice with it before I left, and though I brought the user's manual with me, I didn't ever take the time to study it. So I left the camera on its automatic settings and used it that way during my Camino, taking lots of pictures that I planned to download and share after I returned to the United States.

When I got back home, one of the first things I did was to download the files from my camera, ready to post them on my social media accounts and send to family and friends. But I soon discovered that the files saved by the camera on its automatic settings were MP4 files—the wrong format for what I wanted to do with them.

A friend explained to me that I would need to download a software program that would allow me to watch each video file frame by frame and then save the appropriate frame as a JPG file that I could share on social media. This seemed quite tedious to me, and I was frustrated and impatient. But I did as he suggested, since I had no other choice.

Somewhat to my surprise, I gradually felt my frustration and impatience give way to pleasurable memory as I watched each MP4 file. In the process of reformatting and viewing each file, I realized I was reliving my Camino experience, even remembering things I had forgotten. And once again, I thought, "the Camino is giving me what I need—a belated gift."

Maybe one of the most extreme cases of seeing adversity as a gift came about during a conversation with Kasia (Kate, to her English-speaking friends), a peregrina from Poland. As we walked together from Portomarín to Casanova, she complained about bedbugs. Apparently Kate had been extremely unfortunate to encounter bedbugs in a place where she slept, and she was getting very irritated—in more ways than one.

I said to her, "Well, I can't speak for you, but I'm one of those people who thinks that everything that happens to us on the Camino happens for a reason, and our job is to find out what the gift is, even in unpleasant circumstances."

I can't remember her reply, but a couple of days later, I got a message from her that said, "You were absolutely right. I had to change my perspective to see the gift. It prepared me for the gift that I was about to receive, and had that not happened, the gift I got wouldn't have happened."

It seems that Kate had decided to stop at a particular place, perhaps to find a hot shower and soothe some of her bedbug bites. There she met someone who was very kind to her and gained an important new relationship. I learned all this a year later from a Facebook post Kate made, describing not only the gift of the new relationship, but also an anonymous traveling companion (yours truly) who had suggested that even bedbugs could have a gift to offer if one could only find it.

Of course, unlike my shoe, the camera, and Kate's bedbugs, not every gift comes wrapped in a problem to be solved. I've already spoken about the street musicians in Santo Domingo de la Calzada and the smiling sunflower on the road outside Belorado. These were both instances where I received an unexpected, unplanned gift of joy, just by being alive and present in the moment. And there were dozens, maybe hundreds of other such gifts all along the way.

Benefits of Gratitude

As we all know, when you receive a gift, the proper response is to say thank you. I've already said several times that while I walked the Camino de Santiago, I had an overwhelming sense of gratitude—despite a hole in my shoe, missing a few trail markers, and the ever-present heat of the Spanish summer. This sense of gratitude, no doubt, was central in my ability to both perceive and receive the gifts the Camino presented to me.

But there is strong reason to believe that cultivating "an attitude of gratitude" may offer many other benefits to our psyche and even our physical health. An April 2015 article in *Psychology Today* outlines seven specific benefits of gratitude that have even been validated by scientific research.[14]

According to a 2014 study published in the peer-reviewed journal *Emotion*,[15] expressing gratitude to a new acquaintance increases the likelihood that the individual will desire to continue the relationship. Similar to the "social integration" theory of Susan Pinker's longevity research (Chapter 13),[16] it seems that the simple act of thanking someone can open new opportunities. It makes sense; when your mom kept reminding you to send all those thank-you notes to the people who sent you graduation gifts, she was just trying to help you get a leg up in life!

---

14 Amy Morin, "7 Scientifically Proven Benefits of Gratitude," *Psychology Today*, April 3, 2015, https://www.psychologytoday.com/us/blog/what-mentally-strong-people-dont-do/201504/7-scientifically-proven-benefits-gratitude.

15 Lisa A. Williams and Monica Y. Bartlett, "Warm Thanks: Gratitude Expression Facilitates Social Affiliation in New Relationships Via Perceived Warmth," *Emotion* 15, no. 1 (August 2014): 1–5, https://doi.apa.org/doiLanding?doi=10.1037%2Femo0000017.

16 Pinker, *The Village Effect*.

A 2012 study in *Personality and Individual Differences* indicated that grateful people experience fewer aches and pains and report feeling healthier in general than others.[17] Furthermore, the study suggests that grateful people are also more likely to take care of their health by methods like frequent exercise and seeing their doctor regularly.

Gratitude also seems beneficial in limiting the experience of "toxic emotions" such as regret, envy, and resentment that can undermine emotional health. University of California–Davis researcher Robert Emmons says that gratitude increases happiness and reduces depression.[18]

Grateful people are also more likely to behave in prosocial ways, even when they encounter persons who do not. A 2012 study at the University of Kentucky showed that persons who ranked higher on a psychological measure of gratitude were less likely to retaliate and experienced higher levels of empathy and sensitivity toward others, even when they received negative feedback.[19]

If you want to sleep better, try spending a few minutes before bedtime jotting down things you are thankful for, or good things that happened that day. A 2011 study published in *Applied*

---

17   Patrick L. Hill, Mathias Allemand, and Brent W. Roberts, "Examining the Pathways between Gratitude and Self-rated Physical Health across Adulthood," *Personality and Individual Differences*, January 2013, https://www.sciencedirect.com/science/article/abs/pii/S0191886912004011.

18   Robert Emmons, "Why Gratitude is Good." *Greater Good Magazine*, November 16, 2010, https://greatergood.berkeley.edu/article/item/why_gratitude_is_good.

19   Nathan DeWall, et al., "A Grateful Heart is a Nonviolent Heart: Cross-Sectional, Experience Sampling, Longitudinal, and Experimental Evidence," *Semantic Scholar*, March 1, 2012. https://www.semanticscholar.org/paper/A-Grateful-Heart-is-a-Nonviolent-Heart-DeWall-Lambert/dbe035a2eba8aad922f8843ea02a5f5731a6711e.

Psychology: Health and Well-Being found a strong correlation between gratitude and improved sleep patterns.[20]

The certificate I received from the Pilgrim's Office in Finisterre at the end of my Camino journey. This is most certainly a gift I am grateful for!

---

20   Joshua A. Rash, M. Kyle Matsuba, and Kenneth M. Prkachin, "Gratitude and Well-Being: Who Benefits the Most from a Gratitude Intervention?" *Applied Psychology*, October 27, 2011, https://iaap-journals.onlinelibrary. wiley.com/doi/abs/10.1111/j.1758-0854.2011.01058.x.

According to research published in 2014 in the *Journal of Applied Sport Psychology*,[21] athletes with a strong sense of gratitude had higher self-esteem, a central component in maximum athletic performance. So it seems that to be at your best, it might be wise to find more reasons to be grateful.

Following the horrific 9/11 attacks, people who could find reasons to be grateful were more resilient, according to a study presented in the *Journal of Personality and Social Psychology*.[22] Not only that, but a 2006 survey of Vietnam veterans in *Behavior Research and Therapy* found that those who had higher feelings of gratitude experienced fewer symptoms of post-traumatic stress disorder.[23] Apparently gratitude can make you mentally stronger and more resistant to the negative effects of trauma.

All that said, my guess is that most of us don't need scientific proof to believe that grateful people are happier, healthier, and more resilient than others. In fact, I suspect that most of us, if given the choice, would rather spend time around grateful people than those with a constant negative, cynical view of their surroundings. And once again, research offers evidence

21 Lung Hung Chen and Chiahuei Wu, "Gratitude Enhances Change in Athletes' Self-Esteem: The Moderating Role of Trust in Coach," *Journal of Applied Sport Psychology* 26, no. 3 (May 2014): 349-362 https://www.researchgate.net/publication/271567980_Gratitude_Enhances_Change_in_Athletes'_Self-Esteem_The_Moderating_Role_of_Trust_in_Coach.

22 Barbara L. Fredrickson, Michele M. Tugade, Christian E. Waugh, and Gregory R. Larkin, "What Good are Positive Emotions in Crises? A Prospective Study of Resilience and Emotions Following the Terrorist Attacks on the United States on September 11th, 2001," *Journal of Personality and Social Psychology* 84, no. 2 (February 2003): 365-376, https://www.ncbi.nlm.nih.gov/pmc/articles/PMC2755263/.

23 Todd B. Kashdan, Gitendra Uswatte, and Terri Julian, "Gratitude and Hedonic and Eudaimonic Well-Being in Vietnam War Veterans," *Behavior Research and Therapy* 44, no. 2 (February 2006): 177-199, https://pubmed.ncbi.nlm.nih.gov/16389060/.

that when we perceive gratitude in others, we are motivated to like them and even please them.

A study at the University of Pennsylvania's Wharton School divided fundraising workers randomly into two groups.[24] The first group carried out their duties with no change in procedure or input, but the second group received a pep talk from their director that included thanking them for their efforts. The following week, researchers noted that the second group made 50 percent more calls to potential donors than the group that didn't hear the positive affirmation from the director. Put simply, when others express gratitude for our endeavors, it motivates us to work even harder.

All this persuades me that gratitude itself is a gift—one that tends to replicate itself over and over, both in us and in the people around us who are recipients of our gratitude. When we're grateful, we're more aware of the gifts that come into our lives. And when we celebrate those gifts with gratitude, our "gift-awareness" expands even more. To me, this seems like a supremely positive cycle, one that motivates me to keep my eyes wide open for the gifts that each day offers. I want to put more gratitude into the environment—I think our world needs it.

As I hope is clear to anyone who has read this far, the Camino de Santiago was itself one of the greatest gifts I have ever received in my life. The experience of this ancient pilgrimage has taught me things about myself and others that I could never have learned any other way. Even as this is being written,

---

24   Adam M. Grant, et al., "Impact and the Art of Motivation Maintenance: The Effects of Contact with Beneficiaries on Persistence Behavior," *Organizational Behavior and Human Decision Processes* 103, no. 1 (May 2007): 53-67, https://www.sciencedirect.com/science/article/abs/pii/S0749597806000641.

long after I finished my walk through Spain, the Camino is still teaching me lessons. I suppose I will spend the rest of my life absorbing everything the Camino has given me.

On my thirty-fifth day of walking, as I approached the end of my pilgrimage, the Camino gave me a gift that brought everything home in a way that was both so powerful and so simple that I'm not sure I can adequately explain it. In the next chapter I'm going to give it a try.

For Reflection

- Do you consider yourself a grateful person? What is your opinion of the importance of gratitude in a person's life?

- When you think of reasons for gratitude in your own life, do they tend to be focused on people or on circumstances? What is the difference?

Scan to see a color image of the photos in this chapter.

CHAPTER 15

"Buen Camino"

On August 19, 2018, I walked into the plaza of the Cathedral de Santiago de Compostela—the destination of pilgrims on the Camino. With me were six fellow peregrinos: Philipp, Denise, Astrid from Austria; Luca and Andrea from Italy; and Julia from Germany. Philipp, Astrid, and Julia were three of the members of my original Fellowship, formed at the beginning of the pilgrimage as we left Saint-Jean-Pied-de-Port to cross the Pyrenees into Spain.

Reaching the cathedral, the traditional destination since the Middle Ages, was a peak moment. The air around us was bathed in an ambiance of weariness and excitement, with a dash of relief tossed in. The plaza was full of other pilgrims who had walked hundreds of miles, through heat and rain, in order to arrive at this place. Like us, they had endured blisters, fatigue, and aching muscles. Along the way, they had formed bonds with each other and learned deep lessons about themselves.

The six fellow travelers who arrived in Santiago de Compostela with me. From left to right: Philipp, Denise, Astrid, Luca, Andrea, me, and Julia.

But my walk was not yet finished. I had previously decided that, rather than ending my Camino upon reaching the cathedral, I would continue my journey to Finisterre on the Atlantic coast, about 100 kilometers (approximately sixty-two miles) west of Santiago de Compostela. I will explain more about Finisterre and its significance in the epilogue.

And so, the day after arriving at the cathedral, I got up and started walking to the village of Negreira, my destination for the day, almost fourteen miles away. Though many pilgrims make this final journey to the coast after reaching Santiago de Compostela, the way is generally much less crowded. Also, on this leg, one is likely to meet pilgrims who arrived at the cathedral from one of the other traditional routes, such as the Camino Portugués (the Portuguese Way), the Camino del Norte (the Northern Way), the Camino Primitivo (the Original Way), and others.

On August 23, 2018, my fourth day of walking from Santiago de Compostela and the thirty-fifth day of my pilgrimage since leaving Saint-Jean-Pied-de-Port, I reached Finisterre, my final destination. As I completed the twenty-one miles between Muxía and Finisterre, I happened to see a message, painted on a rock beside the trail.

The meaningful message I saw on August 23, 2018,
that still influences me to this day.

Here is a portion of what I wrote in my Facebook journal for that day:

Day 35 finally came and is now over. When I started planning my Camino, I thought I could walk from Saint-Jean-Pied-de-Port to Santiago de Compostela in 31 days, with an additional four days to walk to Muxía and Finisterre. But to be safe I built five days into my schedule just in case I wanted to take a day off, or if I needed to take a day to allow blisters to heal and aches and pains to diminish.

I am thankful I never had to use my free days for those reasons. I escaped significant blisters and aches and pains. I am surprised that my mind was not screaming at me one single day. This has truly been a great experience. If anyone is contemplating this in the future, I would be glad to talk.

I saw the image you see in this photo on today's 21.11 mile walk from Muxía to Finisterre. "Buen camino" is a phrase pilgrims say to each other and a term many locals say to pilgrims when they walk by. It means, "Walk well; happy trails."

However, when I saw this, it really hit me that today was my last day of purposeful walking on the Camino. It seemed that the Camino's message to me was, "Good-bye, Gordon. Thanks for embracing the spirit of the Camino. Thanks for listening to my messages to you. Walk well as you continue your Camino elsewhere."

I knew today was the last day of walking, but this made it real. It is over, but it continues. I am going to miss the Camino, miss the people who have been important to me during these 35 days, and miss learning about people on the Camino. I am beyond grateful that I had the opportunity to complete this walk on the Camino de Santiago.

It is difficult to explain to someone who has not experienced the Camino de Santiago the rush of emotion that came over me when I saw this simple, hand-painted message on a rock. In fact, to this day, I can scarcely read the words I wrote in my online journal and look at the image without feeling many of those same emotions rising up, constricting my throat and even bringing tears to my eyes.

I know, of course, that I am not the only pilgrim to have such feelings. In fact, many of my Fellowship expressed similar feelings. Upon finishing my Camino, I remember having the thought that I should immediately begin walking to Jerusalem (even though doing that would have been impractical, to say the least).

Joyce Rupp writes, near the conclusion of her book *Walk in a Relaxed Manner*,[25] as she contemplates the ending of her walk on the Camino, "A part of me wants to keep on going, to let the persistent movement take me forward into ever-new vistas and discoveries. Unknowingly, I had become attached to the steady pace of walking. No doubt about it—the pattern and motion of walking claimed me... I assured myself the Camino would continue. The physical part was completed, but the spiritual part, the joys and challenges of the pilgrimage, were only beginning to sink deep roots."

Deep roots indeed. My reaction to the painted "buen camino" message was driven by feelings of gladness for completion of an important goal, and also some portion of sadness—maybe "longing" is a better word—upon understanding that the actual physical process of achievement was coming to an end. But as

---

25 Joyce Rupp, *Walk in a Relaxed Manner: Life Lessons from the Camino* (Ossing, New York: Orbis Books, 2005) p. 253.

214 • *Buen Camino*

I have suggested several times already, my experience on the Camino de Santiago has become for me—to use a phrase first made popular by a 1920s ad for Victor Radio—a gift that keeps on giving.

Scarcely a day goes by when I don't think about or reflect on some aspect of my pilgrimage and what it taught me. As time passes, those roots of reflection, gratitude, self-knowledge, and heightened perception of what is truly important in life only deepen. In fact, by this point, it is almost impossible for me to imagine what my life would have been like had I not walked the Camino de Santiago.

The Attitude of Buen Camino

Psychologists who have studied the science behind our re-actions to goal setting and goal completion have separated objectives into two types: task goals (sometimes referred to as "mastery-learning goals") and ego goals (also called "performance-competitive goals"). The second category en-compasses goals that someone might embark upon in order to set themselves apart from others. An athlete in a race, for example, has a performance-competitive goal of finishing ahead of her competitors. A salesperson in a contest might have a performance-competitive goal of closing more sales than anyone else. Goals in the first category, by contrast, have more to do with self-understanding and self-improvement, such as someone who has set a goal of learning a second language, or a person who embarks on an advanced field of study.

While there is nothing wrong with either type of goal, re-searchers have noted that ego goals are often associated with anxiety, excessive competitiveness, and self-consciousness. On the other hand, task goals are more often associated with interest, commitment, perceived improvement, and life satisfaction. Also notably, ego goals are often more extrinsic in motivation (motivation from outside the self), while task goals tend to have intrinsic motivations (coming from within oneself).

As I mentioned early in the book, my principal goal or objective while walking the Camino was simply to be fully present and aware of each moment as it occurred. Obviously my goal was not competitive or even particularly performative in nature. Rather, as I said earlier, I was more interested in "becoming" than "achieving." If my focus had been solely on walking a certain number of miles and arriving at a certain destination, the Camino would have been nowhere near as meaningful as it was—and continues to be—in my daily life.

This impact is nowhere more important than in my work with clients and team members at Bernhardt Wealth Management. My pilgrimage in Spain taught me, among other things, that cultivating the attitude of "buen camino" enhances the quality of almost every endeavor. When I am truly present with my colleagues, for example, I am better able to perceive and understand their challenges, strengths, and even suggestions for improvement in our work. When I am attentive to each moment I spend with our clients, the result is better empathy, more focused attention to their needs and goals, and improved outcomes in our financial planning and advising work on their behalf.

By truly taking to heart the meaning of "buen camino"—the recognition that we are all on life's journey together, that each of us can make a positive impact on the experience of others, that the responsibility to be a valuable and dependable traveling companion extends to each moment—I believe that I am becoming better, more effective, and more self-aware in every area of life and work.

But there's more. As I have continued to reflect on what the Camino de Santiago meant and continues to mean to me, I have realized that "buen camino" is also a promise: a commitment to every peregrino I meet—whether on a pilgrimage in Spain or in an appointment at my office—to be a useful, dependable companion on the trail of life. As I said in Chapter 4, we're all peregrinos: pilgrims on a journey to a common destination. In every area of my life, and especially in my work with our treasured clients, I am committed to understanding where my fellow travelers are headed and to doing whatever I can to help them arrive safely.

On the Camino de Santiago, challenges are inevitable: blisters, fatigue, heat, thirst, and even unintended detours and broken shoes can increase the difficulty of successfully completing the journey. You can easily make the connection to our walk through life: business and career setbacks, bear markets, illness, divorce, and death are obstacles that almost every traveler must face at one time or another. And yet the promise of "buen camino" assures us that our trusted fellow travelers are there with us to encourage, support, and help us find the way when we wander off the trail.

In Chapter 12, I described the challenge coin I designed some years ago, with the image of my mother's piano on one side and the name of our firm on the other. My further reflections on my pilgrimage in Spain eventually inspired me to have another coin created: one that reminds me and, I hope, others of the deeper meaning behind the phrase "buen camino."

The new Bernhardt Wealth Management Challenge Coin,
effective as of the publication of this book.

On one side of the coin is a scallop shell, the image of the Camino de Santiago pilgrimage that symbolizes each individual peregrino who walks the trail and the trail itself, as indicated by its use as a waymarker for travelers. The image of the shell is accompanied by the word "fiduciary," which sums up our professional and ethical commitment to always, in everything, do what is in the client's best interest. On the other side of the coin is our company logo, accompanied by the Four Cs: Character, Chemistry, Caring, and Competence.

As we distribute these coins to clients and other people who are important to us, our hope is that both the giver and receiver are reminded of the wish and the promise contained in "buen camino": we not only hope that our fellow travelers are journeying well, but we are also committed to walk beside them and do what we can to make the journey successful, enjoyable, and satisfying.

There is a passage in the New Testament book of James that captures the spirit of our intentions. It says, "Suppose a brother or sister is without clothes or daily food. If one of you says to them, 'Go in peace; keep warm and well fed,' but does nothing about their physical needs, what good is it?" In other words, "buen camino," for us, goes beyond well wishes or good intentions; it signifies a promise to do whatever we can to aid, support, and encourage our fellow pilgrims.

You may have heard the maxim, "The biggest room in the world is the room for improvement." Living each day of life with the moment-by-moment attitude of "buen camino" has placed me on a deeply satisfying journey toward improvement, not only of myself, but of the world around me, and especially my relationships with and usefulness for the people in my life: my family, friends, work colleagues, and clients. I have learned that "buen camino" is so much more than a greeting between travelers; it is a way of life.

For Reflection

- When you think of what has given you the most meaning in your life, what comes to mind?

- If recognizing the humanity of others is important, what are some ways we can do that each day?

Scan to see a color image of the photos in this chapter.

A Walk to the
End of the World

Upon reaching Santiago de Compostela on August 19, 2018, I went to the Oficina de Acogida al Peregrino (Pilgrims' Reception Office) to obtain the final stamp on my pilgrim passport and also my "Compostela": the official certificate documenting my completion of the Camino de Santiago. But as I mentioned in the last chapter, even though I was now "official," I knew I had an additional journey ahead in order to arrive at my intended final destination.

The next morning, as I noted in the last chapter, I set off for the final leg of my pilgrimage. I was bound for Finisterre ("Fisterra" in the local Galician dialect), the town on the rugged Atlantic coast that takes its name from Latin, *finis terrae*: "the end of the world."

Less than 10 percent of those who walk the Camino de Santiago undertake the additional journey from Santiago de Compostela to Finisterre. For many, this is because of the time they have allotted for their walk. Having reached the traditional destination of the cathedral, they must return to their jobs, families, and everyday lives. For others, getting to Finisterre just isn't that important.

My Compostela, issued as proof (in Latin) that I completed the required distance on foot as a pilgrim on the Camino de Santiago.

But for me, the idea of walking all the way to the "end of the world" on the Atlantic Coast was important. I had planned to walk thirty-one days to Santiago de Compostela, and the walk felt incomplete if I didn't take an additional four days to say I had walked to the "end of the world" where the land meets the sea.

LAND OF THE DEAD

Finisterre is located on a cape along the Costa da Morte ("the Coast of Death"), so named because of the treacherous rocks that line this section of the coastline, which have caused many shipwrecks through the ages. Tradition holds there was a pagan altar to the sun ("Ara Solis") on the rocky bluff overlooking the Atlantic, where a lighthouse now stands. Pre-Christian beliefs held that this was where the land of the living bordered the land of the dead. The colonizing Romans conceived of this place as the westernmost point of Iberian Gaul, which accounts for their thinking of it as "the end of the world." However, Cabo da Roca, near Lisbon, Portugal, is actually farther west.

On the first day, I walked about thirteen and a half miles, from Santiago de Compostela to Negreira. This was one of the shortest walks of my pilgrimage, but it was a tough day for some reason. In my online journal, I blamed part of my difficulty on the heat, and part on the fact that the soles of my shoes were getting thin as I neared the end of my journey. However, the next day I walked almost twenty-three miles from Negreira to Olveiroa, and I felt much better. It was still hot, but for whatever reason, the walking seemed easier.

On August 22, 2018, I arrived in Muxía, on the Atlantic coast. At last I could say that I had walked all the way from the French border to the Atlantic Ocean.

This stone cross stands on the highest point in Muxía, overlooking the harbor. At the base of the cross are items left as "offerings" by peregrinos: shoes, articles of clothing, and other objects.

On August 23, 2018, I finished my journey in Finisterre. I've already mentioned the strong emotions I experienced, realizing that my walk in Spain had reached its end. Without question, this moment has had a similarly profound effect on pilgrims for centuries. Over the ages, it became customary for peregrinos at the end of their pilgrimage to burn their clothing or give it away as a symbol of the transformation they had experienced. Some pilgrims still do this, though nowadays, the burning is limited to isolated instances on the beach at night. Still, many pilgrims choose to leave something behind, either at Muxía or

Finisterre, as a memento or dedication commemorating their experience. As I mentioned previously, I left my shoes at the base of a pilgrim statue in Finisterre.

The lighthouse and hotel in Finisterre. When one is standing here and looking out over the vastness of the Atlantic Ocean, it is easy to understand why the Romans thought this was "the end of the world."

But if you looked carefully at the image of my shoes at the base of the statue (Chapter 14), you may have noticed they were missing shoestrings. As a keepsake, I chose to remove them from the shoes that had carried me so faithfully and well along my path from France to "the end of the world." In addition to the bountiful memories I took with me from my pilgrimage, I wanted to bring home some physical reminders as well.

After I got home, I constructed a shadow box that combined important elements of my pilgrimage into a meaningful memento. In addition to my pilgrim passport exhibiting the colorful stamps from the various places I stopped along the way, the shadow box holds my pilgrim scallop shell, my Saint James cross, another pilgrim cross I received during a pilgrim mass at the cathedral in Hontanas, and my shoelaces. One lace is bundled and mounted at the top left, and the other is arranged to spell out "Camino."

*My shadow box; the one object that I would grab if
my house were on fire since it is irreplaceable.*

Every time I look at the shadow box, it summons a host of memories and other thoughts of my pilgrimage to "the end of the world." But more importantly, it reminds me of what is most important about living in "my world" every day. I can't think about the Camino without remembering how important it is to "walk well," both for myself and for others.

We Are All Fellow Travelers

And so, as we reach the end of this journey together, I can hardly do better, by way of parting words, than to return to the ideas with which I started this book. We are all fellow travelers, whether we are walking together on a road in Spain, working in tandem toward a goal in a business, or living side by side in a family. We have come from many different places, but we are all trying to reach the same place: understanding and fitting into our place in this world and in the lives of those dearest to us. All of us, whether we realize it or not, are on a journey toward self-understanding, significance, and meaning.

I hope that you are not only aware of your journey but also deeply committed to it. I hope that you are able to see the exceeding value of each moment and that you can receive the gifts that each day brings. Above all, I hope that your journey goes well.

Buen camino!

Scan to see a color image of the photos in this chapter.

Gordon's Daily Schedule on the Camino de Santiago

I departed from the Washington Dulles International Airport at 5:25 p.m. on July 17, 2018, and arrived at the Charles de Gaulle International Airport in Paris at 6:55 a.m. on July 18. The next day I took a train and bus to Saint-Jean-Pied-de-Port in southwestern France, in the foothills of the Pyrenees. The following day I took my first steps on the Camino de Santiago and continued walking from town to town as noted below:

July 20—Saint-Jean-Pied-de-Port to Roncesvalles

July 21—Roncesvalles to Zubiri

July 22—Zubiri to Pamplona

July 23—Pamplona to Puente la Reina

July 24—Puente la Reina to Estella

July 25—Estella to Los Arcos

July 26—Los Arcos to Logroño

July 27—Logroño to Nájera

July 28—Nájera to Santo Domingo de la Calzada

July 29—Santo Domingo de la Calzada to Belorado

July 30—Belorado to San Juan de Ortega

July 31—San Juan de Ortega to Burgos

August 1—Burgos to Hontanas

August 2—Hontanas to Boadilla del Camino

August 3—Boadilla del Camino to Carrión de los Condes

August 4—Carrión de los Condes to Moratinos

August 5—Moratinos to Calzadilla de los Hermanillos

August 6—Calzadilla de los Hermanillos to León

August 8—León to Villavante

August 9—Villavante to Astorga

August 10—Astorga to Foncebadón

August 11—Foncebadón to Ponferrada

August 12—Ponferrada to Villafranca del Bierzo

August 13—Villafranca del Bierzo to O'Cebreiro

August 14—O'Cebreiro to Triacastela

August 15—Triacastela to Sarria

August 16—Sarria to Portomarín

August 17—Portomarín to Casanova

August 18—Casanova to Salceda

August 19—Salceda to Santiago de Compostela

August 20—Santiago de Compostela to Negreira

August 21—Negreira to Olveiroa

August 22—Olveiroa to Muxía

August 23—Muxía to Finisterre

I spent August 24 enjoying the views from Finisterre and caught a bus back to Santiago de Compostela the next day. I had three days to enjoy the city before I caught a train to Madrid. I departed Adolfo Suárez Madrid-Barajas Airport at 11:15 a.m.

on August 30, and arrived at Washington Dulles International Airport on August 30 at 2:00 p.m. I stopped by the office and shared a "Santiago cake" with my teammates before I walked home. I walked to the office on September 4 for my first day of work on-site since I left in July.

The Bernhardt Way

Choosing a trusted wealth manager is more than just a business decision. It's a personal one as well. At Bernhardt Wealth Management, we believe in creating relationships built on a foundation of trust in order to make the maximum possible impact in the lives of our clients. We believe trust is earned and is the most important asset we manage. We create trusting, long-term relationships by focusing on 4 Cs: Character, Chemistry, Caring, and Competence. But what do these words mean in daily practice? The twenty-six Fundamentals that follow provide the answer. They're what set us apart and what make us leaders in our field. We call it The Bernhardt Way.

1. **Put clients first, always.** We exist to serve our clients' best interests. Period. We have a fiduciary responsibility to make sure that our advice is free of any biases and that we avoid any conflict of interest. When people give us their money, we enter into a sacred trust with them. Honor that trust ALWAYS.

2. **Make quality personal.** Take pride in the quality of everything you touch and everything you do. From the way you create a proposal to the way you answer the phone, from the way you research a solution to the way you fill out paperwork, always ask yourself, "Is this my best work?" Remember that everything you touch has your signature. **Sign in bold ink.**

3. **Practice transparency.** We sell trust more than we sell anything else, and nothing helps build trust more than practicing transparency. Be completely transparent about our relationships, our fees, and even what we can and cannot do.

4. **Attend to details.** Accuracy is everything in our business. Be in the habit of proofreading all letters, e-mails, spreadsheets and proposals for accuracy and correctness. The goal is to get things "right," not simply to get things "done." Being obsessively careful about the details is a demonstration of how much we care.

5. **Honor commitments.** Do what you say you're going to do, when you say you're going to do it. This includes being on time for all phone calls, appointments, meetings and promises. If a commitment can't be fulfilled, notify others early and agree on a new timeframe to be honored.

6. **Be a fanatic about response time.** People expect us to respond to their questions and concerns quickly, whether

it's in person, on the phone or by e-mail. This includes simply acknowledging that we got the question and we're "on it," as well as keeping those involved continuously updated on the status of outstanding issues. Rapid response keeps us standing out from the crowd.

7. **Execute due diligence.** Developing the best solution for the client isn't always obvious and isn't always easy. Often it requires significant research as well as creativity. Have a bias for thoroughness and do the extra work necessary to find the best way to meet the client's objectives.

8. **Care like it's your family.** Clients don't care how much we know until they know how much we care. Do the small things (handwritten notes, cards, phone calls) that show people you're paying attention to them as individuals and that you genuinely care. Treat them with the compassion you would a member of your own family.

9. **Listen generously.** Listening is more than simply "not speaking." Give others your undivided attention. Be present and engaged. Quiet the noise in your head and let go of the need to agree or disagree. Suspend your judgment and be curious to know more, rather than jumping to conclusions. Above all, listen to *understand*.

10. **Speak straight.** Speak honestly in a way that helps to make progress. Say what you mean, and be willing to ask questions, share ideas, or raise issues that may cause conflict when it's necessary for team success. Have the

courage to say what needs to be said. Address issues directly with those who are involved or affected.

11. **Practice blameless problem-solving.** Just fix it. Demonstrate a relentless solution focus, rather than pointing fingers or dwelling on problems. Identify lessons learned and use those lessons to improve ourselves and our processes so we don't make the same mistake twice. Learn from every experience.

12. **Get clear on expectations.** We judge situations not by what happens, but by how they compare to what we expected to happen. Create clarity and avoid misunderstandings by discussing expectations upfront. Set expectations for others and ask when you're not clear on what they expect of you.

13. **Make each interaction count.** Every contact with a client is an opportunity to create a positive experience. This includes calls, visits, voicemail, letters, e-mails, and every other communication. Make sure every interaction leaves our client feeling wanted, appreciated and respected.

14. **Find a way.** Take personal responsibility for solving problems and making things happen—*somehow, someway.* Take ownership and respond to every situation by looking for how it *can* be done, rather than explaining why it can't. Work with a sense of urgency. Be resourceful and show initiative.

15. **Communicate to be understood.** Comprehension is the responsibility of the communicator, so know your audience. Write and speak in a way that they can understand. Avoid using industry acronyms and jargon. Use the simplest possible explanations.

16. **Help get it done.** Our goal isn't simply to "discuss" issues or to "explore" possibilities. Rather, it's to help our clients *solve* their most important financial planning challenges. Follow-up everything and take responsibility to see that clients come to completion in resolving their pressing issues.

17. **Offer meaningful appreciation.** Recognizing people doing things right is more effective than pointing out when they do things wrong. Regularly extend *meaningful* acknowledgment and appreciation—in all directions throughout our organization.

18. **Create win/win solutions.** Success is a two-way street. Learn to think from the other person's perspective. Discover what others need and find a way to help them meet those needs while also fulfilling your own. Win/win solutions are always more effective and longer lasting than win/lose situations.

19. **Invest in relationships.** Everything we do is built on trust and trust is built on relationships. Make smart decisions that enhance long-term relationships. Be fair with clients and our partners. Strong relationships enable us

to more successfully work through difficult issues and challenging times.

20. **Assume positive intent.** Work from the assumption that people are good, fair, and honest, and that the intent behind their actions is positive. Set aside your own judgments and preconceived notions. Give people the benefit of the doubt.

21. **Relentlessly improve.** "Because we've always done it that way" is not a reason. Regularly consider every aspect of your job to find ways to improve. Try a new approach. Look at it from a unique perspective. Think differently. Share what you learn so that others can benefit from best practices as well.

22. **Look ahead and anticipate.** Solve problems *before* they happen by anticipating future issues, planning for contingencies, and addressing them in advance. Work with appropriate lead times. Preventing issues is always better than fixing them.

23. **Take pride in our appearance.** Your personal appearance makes a strong statement about the pride you take in your performance. Dress neatly and professionally. The appearance of our office makes a similar statement about the quality of our work. Take responsibility to see that our office environment is clean, neat, and professional.

24. **Be a team player.** Don't let ego or personal agenda get in the way of doing what's best for the team. Be there for each other and be willing to step into another role or help a co-worker when that's what's required for success. *We win and lose as a team.*

25. **Give back. Pay it forward.** Regularly seek opportunities to assist those in need. Express genuine gratitude for the help received by paying it forward and helping others. Be a servant leader and put the needs of others ahead of your own.

26. **Keep it fun.** While our passion for excellence is real, remember that the world has bigger problems than the daily challenges that make up our work. Stuff happens. Keep perspective. Don't take things personally or take yourself too seriously. Laugh every day.

Twelve Essential Insights for Building Wealth: A Summary

At various places in this book I have referred to basic principles of investment and investor psychology that guide our advisory and management work with the clients of Bernhardt Wealth Management. The following summary includes twelve key factors that we work to instill in our approach to managing clients' investment portfolios. We also try to educate our clients on the importance of these underlying principles as foundational to long-term investing success.

1. **You, the Market, and the Prices You Pay:** Understanding group intelligence and its effect on efficient market pricing is a first step toward more consistently buying low and selling high in free capital markets.

2. **Ignoring the Siren Song of Daily Market Pricing:** Rather than trying to react to ever-changing conditions and cutthroat competition, invest your life savings according to factors over which you can expect to have some control.

3. **Financial Gurus and Other Fantastic Creatures:** Avoid paying costly, speculative "experts" to pinch-hit your market moves for you. The evidence indicates that their ability to persistently beat the market is more likely to be fleeting than fantastic.

4. **The "Full-Meal Deal" of Diversification:** In place of speculative investing, diversification is among your most important allies. To begin with, spreading your assets around dampens unnecessary risks while potentially improving overall expected returns.

5. **Managing the Market's Risky Business:** All risks are not created equal. Unrewarded "concentrated risks" (picking individual stocks) can and should be avoided by diversifying away from it. "Market-related risks" (holding swaths of the market) are expected to deliver long-term returns. Diversification helps manage the necessary risks involved.

6. **Get Along, Little Market:** Diversification can also create a smoother ride through bumpy markets, which helps you stay on track toward your personal goals.

7. **The Business of Investing:** At their essence, market returns are compensation for providing the financial capital that feeds the human enterprise going on all around us.

8. **The Essence of Evidence-Based Investing:** What separates solid evidence from flaky findings? Evidence-based insights demand scholarly rigor, including an objective outlook, robust peer review, and the ability to reproduce similar analyses under varying conditions.

9. **Factors That Figure in Your Evidence-Based Portfolio:** Following where nearly seventy years of robust evidence-based inquiry has taken us so far, three key stock market factors (equity, value, and small-cap) plus a couple more for bonds (term and credit) have formed a backbone for evidence-based portfolio construction.

10. **What Has Evidence-Based Investing Done for Me Lately?** Building on our understanding of which market factors seem to matter the most, we continue to heed unfolding evidence on best investment practices.

11. **The Human Factor in Evidence-Based Investing:** The most significant factor for investors may be the human factor. Behavioral finance helps us understand that our own instinctive reactions to market events can overtake any other market challenges we face.

12. **Behavioral Biases—What Makes Your Brain Trick (You)?** Continuing our exploration of behavioral finance, we share a half-dozen deep-seated instincts that can trick you into making significant money-management mistakes. Here, perhaps more than anywhere else, an objective, professional, fiduciary advisor can help you avoid mishaps that your own myopic vision might miss.

A LIFE OF GRATITUDE

Thank-Yous and Acknowledgments

To my parents: I got my mother's smile and compassion, and my father's work ethic. The values I hold most dear are those you instilled in me. I am thankful for your unconditional love and the virtues you exemplified for me: honesty, character, and a commitment to helping others. I wouldn't be half the man I am today without your influence. Thank you. And Mom, even though we lost you in 2006, we think of you often.

To my sisters—Devonne, Gloria, and Barb: You have always believed in me. I often think that you were better sisters to me than I was a brother to you. I appreciate how you always enhanced the relationships I have with your children. I was also blessed with an older sister, Donell, who was taken from this world so long ago. I appreciate and value each one of you. Thank you.

Thank you to each and every one of my high school teachers. Growing up with a graduating class of thirty-one, you know everyone, and all the teachers know every student. I especially appreciate Mrs. Rawalt. We were first introduced during an assembly when we freshman boys were a little too noisy. While she was trying to make the point that she was not happy with our behavior, I gave her a big smile. Unbeknownst to her, my nickname was Smiley, and smiling was just my natural state. But on this day my smile only served to irritate her. We eventually got to know each other better and often laughed about this first encounter. Deeply committed to all her students, she never failed to encourage me and tell me how proud she was of my accomplishments. I made a point of visiting her whenever I returned to Nebraska, including a surprise appearance at her ninetieth birthday celebration. High school was a long time ago, but I continue to appreciate the lasting impact of Mrs. Rawalt and each of my high school teachers.

I thank every person who has worked at Bernhardt Wealth Management—past and current—for their vital role in my development as a business leader. I owe my partners, Tim Koehl, Solon Vlasto, and Bonnie Maingault, a debt of gratitude for never abandoning me when I made mistakes and for patiently enduring the evolution of my leadership. Without my partners and teammates, I never would have dreamed that I could disconnect from the business for forty-nine days to undertake the most incredible experience of my life. Thank you for caring for our clients and each other and making this possible.

I want to thank the clients of Bernhardt Wealth Management. The trust and faith you have placed in us deepens the honor I feel in serving you with the fiduciary care we all take so seriously. Recording a thank-you video on my company's anniversary while I was on the Camino was a very emotional moment for me, as I became too choked up to speak. I was overcome by such deep feelings of gratitude for you that I had to make several attempts to record the message. My appreciation for you is genuinely heartfelt, and I know my trip would not have been possible without you. Thank you for the honor of serving you.

To the Fellowship: I began my journey alone, not knowing who I would meet and wondering if perhaps I'd walk for thirty-five days in solitude. Thankfully I met Julia from Germany, Philipp from Austria, Szandra and Petra from Hungary, and Astrid and Tanja from Austria, on my first day of walking in the Pyrenees. In a nod to *The Lord of the Rings*, I called you my "Fellowship." It was always a joy to see you and share stories. Although Petra and Tanja had to return home early, I was glad to reach Santiago de Compostela with Astrid, Philipp, and Julia, and then happily reconnected with Szandra in Finisterre. I met numerous peregrinos along my journey and was enriched by each encounter, but my "Fellowship" was one of the greatest gifts I received on the Camino. Thank you for your support and friendship. I was blessed to encounter you on my first day of walking.

I have been a Vistage member since 2009, and it has been one of the best investments I have ever made in my leadership development. I value the relationships and friendships I have developed with my Vistage peers in CE Group 3643, the many other Vistage members I have met, and the many Vistage chairs in the Washington, DC area. Knowing you has inspired me to be a better leader and having accountability partners in 3643 has been immensely beneficial. Thank you. I especially want to thank Vistage Master Chair and fellow peregrino Peter Schwartz for his leadership, friendship, and coaching. I wouldn't be the same person without you.

One of my best talents is the ability to listen, and I've used that skill to discover the stories of over 700 executive leaders. Hearing about your influences, defining moments, and leadership philosophies has made me an even better leader. Thank you for trusting me to share your stories in the Profiles in Success series.

I want to thank two people who helped me find the words to articulate the most consequential experience of my life. Understanding just how important the Camino de Santiago is to me, you were both hugely influential throughout the development of this book. Thank you, Thom Lemmons and Karen Embry, for impacting the quality of my storytelling.

To the readers who have invested in this book: Whether you have an interest in the Camino de Santiago or are seeking a reliable wealth guide on your financial journey through life, I wish you peace and success on your journey. Thank you, and buen camino.

Thank you to everyone at Scribe Media who helped take this book to market, especially CEO JeVon McCormick, publishing manager Erin Mellor, editor Alan Gintzler, editor-in-chief Hal Clifford, designer Michael Nagin, and copywriter Erin Michelle Skye, the QA team Simon Kerr, Callie Berringer, and Caroline Hough.

To all others who provided encouragement, feedback, and reviews throughout the writing process: Thank you for helping to make this a better book.

CPSIA information can be obtained
at www.ICGtesting.com
Printed in the USA
BVHW081944021022
648364BV00005B/21/J

9 781544 532226